To My Dearest Teresa.
You are truly me sister in Christ.
Love you.
Link Jackie

The Secrets of the Glass Slippers

God's Fulfilling Approach to Love & Marriage

Janice G. Johnson

WESTBOW
PRESS®
A DIVISION OF THOMAS NELSON
& ZONDERVAN

Copyright © 2019 Janice G. Johnson.

All rights reserved. No part of this book may be used or reproduced by any means, graphic, electronic, or mechanical, including photocopying, recording, taping or by any information storage retrieval system without the written permission of the author except in the case of brief quotations embodied in critical articles and reviews.

Antoine Smith, Lead Photographer.
Imani O. Johnson, CEO, Maven Market, LLC., Brand Strategist.

This is a work of fiction. All of the characters, names, incidents, organizations, and dialogue in this novel are either the products of the author's imagination or are used fictitiously with the exception of the testimonials.

Unless otherwise noted, all scripture is from the King James Version of the Bible.

WestBow Press books may be ordered through booksellers or by contacting:

WestBow Press
A Division of Thomas Nelson & Zondervan
1663 Liberty Drive
Bloomington, IN 47403
www.westbowpress.com
1 (866) 928-1240

Because of the dynamic nature of the Internet, any web addresses or links contained in this book may have changed since publication and may no longer be valid. The views expressed in this work are solely those of the author and do not necessarily reflect the views of the publisher, and the publisher hereby disclaims any responsibility for them.

Any people depicted in stock imagery provided by Getty Images are models, and such images are being used for illustrative purposes only. Certain stock imagery © Getty Images.

ISBN: 978-1-9736-5463-6 (sc)
ISBN: 978-1-9736-5462-9 (hc)
ISBN: 978-1-9736-5464-3 (e)

Library of Congress Control Number: 2019902375

Print information available on the last page.

WestBow Press rev. date: 04/25/2019

Contents

Acknowledgments vii
Introduction ix
Preface xi

Chapter 1   The Virtuous Princess 1
Chapter 2   The Strengthened Princess 27
Chapter 3   The Purposeful Princess 46
Chapter 4   The Transformed Princess 63
Chapter 5   The Delivered Princess 72
Chapter 6   The Chosen Princess 92
Chapter 7   The Blessed Princess 103

Testimonials 123
About the Author 133

Acknowledgments

All honor, glory and praise to God Almighty for the marvelous things that He has done, is doing and for all that is to come. Thank you to my Lord and Savior, Jesus Christ, for the opportunity to share this letter of love, romance, and marriage in a most beautiful way. I would like to thank my beloved grandmother Inez for teaching me how to love others unconditionally. Most of all, I would like to thank her for teaching me how to pray and how to nurture a loving relationship with God. I thank God for blessing me with two amazing children, Imani and Antoine, who have helped me develop into the woman that I am today. To my beloved mother, Sheila who is now with our Heavenly Father; my amazing stepmother, Olga; and my awesome mother-in-law, Jane, My three Queens, I salute you! Never have I seen such class, elegance, dignity, and power in three women as I see in you. Thank you for filling my life with light, laughter, and love. God bless my dear, departed husband, Napoleon, who is with the Lord and surely resting in peace. Thank you to my pastor Rev. Dr. Lester W. Taylor, Jr., and First Lady Minister Gayle Taylor of Community Baptist Church of Englewood, New Jersey for taking the time to listen to my concept for this book and for encouraging me to continue writing. To my church family who blanket me with love and beautiful friendships, I first fell in love with you while standing on the Sunday morning line to attend the 3rd service of the day. Thank you to my Sisters in Christ who love me unconditionally. You inspire and encourage me. I love you all, and I tell you all the time, so you know who you are. To my talented editor Jacqueline Renee, thank you so much for your contribution and dedication to this book.

> The Spirit of the Lord GOD *is* upon Me,
> Because the Lord has anointed Me
> To preach good tidings to the poor;
> He has sent Me to heal the brokenhearted,
> To proclaim liberty to the captives,
> And the opening of the prison to *those who are* bound;
> To proclaim the acceptable year of the Lord,
> And the day of vengeance of our God;
> To comfort all who mourn,
> To console those who mourn in Zion,
> To give them beauty for ashes,
> The oil of joy for mourning,
> The garment of praise for the spirit of heaviness;
> That they may be called trees of righteousness,
> The planting of the LORD, that He may be glorified.
>
> —Isaiah 61:1–3 (NKJV)

Introduction

Ladies, for generations we have enjoyed the lovely and timeless story of Cinderella with breathtaking excitement. We have fostered and nurtured a deep burning desire to have a prince sweep us off of our feet so that we too may live happily ever after. We have fantasized, and role played the anticipated day that marks our personal encounter with, 'The Prince!' Many women have spent their entire adult lives seeking the man of their dreams. Through the analysis of the Cinderella metaphor and with God's instruction, consider that God wants us to pursue real love from a Biblical, realistic, holistic and spiritual approach. Within this story are specific keys of wisdom and Bible truths that contain the secrets to having the desires of our hearts in love but, we have to do it God's way. God created the institution of marriage, and He knows the joy and pain of marriage. He knows, 'The One' whom he has set aside just for you. God has hand selected your prince. Don't allow another minute to pass you by without understanding God's views on love and how to better attract the prince that God has chosen for you. The tools in this book will prepare you for more meaningful relationships and provide you with a greater understanding of the value of a godly man. I am here to encourage you to become the woman of God that you have been called to be in order to attract that anointed man of God whom the Lord has chosen for you so that you may both advance God's kingdom. So in the interim, shift your focus towards God, work on your personal growth and development while investing quality time into yourself. Practice self-care and self-love as you grow with greater spiritual knowledge and understanding. Don't miss this moment; there is wisdom here for the journey ahead that can save you time, energy, money, and your youth. Experience the true revelation of biblical wisdom that can preserve your mental and physical health and maybe even save your life. Godly wisdom mixed with intuition and spiritual insight will position you to be found by, 'The One' whom He has chosen for you. You've tried everything else, now try it God's way.

Preface

Within the lovely and timeless story of Cinderella are many beautiful, spiritual keys to a better understanding of God's desire for his children regarding love, romance, and marriage. Through spiritual eyes, we will experience God's perspective of love in this bedtime story that still intrigues millions. As we explore the highlights of Cinderella's journey to happily ever after, I will share the spiritual insight found in this story, which I call glass slipper wisdom. It is through this spiritual insight and revelation that we will see why at times our approach to love may not be God's best for us. We will realize that some of our love connections are certainly not built on the everlasting rock of love that God intended for us to experience.

By the end of this story, you will experience that God truly understands the heart of a woman. It is God's sincere desire for his children to be blessed with true love. It is through the institution of marriage that God blesses each couple with a gift of pleasure, intimacy, and companionship for the length of their union. Our God understands the hunt and the passion with which women and men pursue each other. He sees the price of compromise that women sometimes pay to have men in their lives. God knows that every man whom women title as a prince or every woman whom men label as a princess, are not indeed of kingdom quality.

As you turn the pages of this book, consider your approach to finding love and attracting the one whom God desires for you. Be inspired and know that God wants each of us to have a companion who loves, respects, honors, and cares for us. God does not want His children pursuing the imposture prince and princess, but a man of God prince and a virtuous woman princess. God wants His royal couple to find true love and experience a love that is based on His word. Understand that your love connection should be built upon honor, trust, obedience, and love for God.

One thing is for certain, we serve a jealous God, and He must come first in our lives. Many people make the huge mistake of putting man and things before God. God wants to come first in our lives. When we put God first and we prove that He is all that we need it opens doors for miracles. We will also examine one of the greatest love stories ever written in the Bible. We will explore their relationship closer as we study the ways of God in love and romance. In any event, you will not view "happily ever after" the same again. The magic of this fairytale is nothing more than evidence that it is God's desire to see each of us step into happily ever after with a loving and caring companion.

As you read this story, ask God for wisdom, knowledge, revelation, and understanding regarding your own love story. So many times, we seek love from a place of feelings, emotions, insecurities, and even desperation. Let's take the time now to ask God for wisdom and understanding in the areas of love, romance, and marriage. Before you turn another page of this book, please ask God to speak to your heart and open your spiritual mind with wisdom to approach love in a new, promising and fulfilling way. The Bible says in James 1:5 (NIV), "If any of you lacks wisdom, you should ask God, who gives generously to all without finding fault and it will be given to you." Now, let's get comfortable, and explore these glass slipper secrets together.

chapter 1

The Virtuous Princess

Who can find a virtuous wife? For her worth is far above rubies.

—Proverbs 31:10 (NKJV)

Secret #1: If you desire to be a wife, prepare to be a wife.

The story tells us that Cinderella's father was a king. She was his princess and he loved his daughter dearly. He was an exceptional role model and a great measure of a man for her to look up to. She knew exactly what type of man would win her heart one day; she would marry a man who loved and respected her just as her father had done. Cinderella's father cared for her and ensured that he took care of her needs. She was very special to him. Most of you may have been exposed to a rendition of the Cinderella story that excluded her origin. Let me give you some insight into the beginnings of the original Cinderella story. She was the apple of his eyes, the sunshine of his life, and the song in his heart. He indulged his daughter, and he favored her so that she should have her heart's desires. Cinderella was loved by many, and she lived a life of privilege with access to the finer things in life. She was surrounded by exciting and interesting people. She was blessed with favor and grace. Her father wanted the best of everything for her. He set a precedent for her to expect only the best from men who were interested in her. Cinderella's father ensured that she knew who she was and whose she was.

When your father is loving and caring, it may be easier to love God. Women who have been fortunate to experience a loving and warm relationship with their earthly father, may not have such a difficult time trusting God as those who did not. Today, many young girls find it difficult to trust God when the only father they ever knew abandoned the family, mistreated the family, abused them, or never had healthy relationships with them. Understandably, such women wonder whether they can trust God because the father that they knew was not there. In some homes, the father lives there but is not present in terms of loving, interacting and caring for the children. This type of relationship could possibly force a little girl to wonder, "Will God love me and then abandon me? Does God really care? Will I have to do anything that I don't want to do to gain His love and attention?" Unfortunately, many women who were abandoned by their fathers earlier in their lives are not capable of having healthy relationships with men. Most of the time, these women are not aware that the issues of abandonment, rejection and insecurity have a direct affect on their relationship with God. A poor image of a father can be transferred to the image that we have of God. Sometimes it takes many years before women become aware that they have treated God the way their father treated them. Although it may not be intentional, father issues can easily be transferred to future relationships. For many, it creates a vicious cycle of not being able to trust anyone, God included. For some women, such distrust is highlighted and perpetuated within the intimacy of love. Such distrust sometimes surfaces in marriages, relationships, or friendships as contention and disharmony. Ultimately, this creates an atmosphere that lacks intimacy within the relationship. It can also create intimacy problems in a relationship with God. He wants His daughters to have an uninhibited loving and intimate relationship with Him. Some women cannot open their hearts to love or submit to God because past experiences of hurt and pain have caused blockages. Until God is allowed to go in and perform spiritual surgery to clear the blockage that is preventing His daughters from being made whole, they will continue to live in a mental prison of distrust.

The subliminal feeling of expected abandonment ultimately brings about constant and nagging thoughts of distrust and insecurity. A father figure is definitely the yardstick by which a woman can measure the worth of a man. When a father is absent or unavailable, he is creating a void that his daughter may try to fill for the rest of her life. Some women who grow up without a father figure have difficulty choosing men of substance who have good character and are stable life partners. The irony of this situation is that more times than not, these women end up marrying someone who is exactly like the parent whom they misunderstood or struggled with the most. There is no doubt that an absent father creates a void in a child's life. For boys, the void is validation, acceptance, and learning how to be a man— and most important, how to be a good man. Many men live a significant portion of their lives unable to show any emotion, feelings, or compassion for others. So many men pray for the day that they can express their emotional sides without being judged. Young ladies need to see their fathers present in the home, providing for their families, respecting their mothers, and loving and caring for their girls. If a girl sees her father being distant or disrespectful towards her mother, then she learns to engage in aloof and emotionally distant relationships. It is so unfortunate but, those fathers who could have made a positive impact in their daughters' lives did not do so. In turn, these women grow up seeking the approval and validation that they never received from their fathers from the world. They seek a special love from those who are not capable of loving others because they do not love themselves. You cannot give what you do not have. And so, the phrase is coined; "Looking for love in all the wrong places."

Many young ladies grow up to become women with diminished senses of self, low self-confidence, and low self-esteem. We are the products of our past and can only do better when we know better.

When a man approaches a woman who is confident and has standards by which she conducts herself, he must rise to the occasion. A man who cannot relate to such a woman is usually intimidated by her strength or threatened by her power. This woman knows who she is and she is certainly not suffering from any identity crisis.

She is not easily fooled by any games, and she will not tolerate foolishness. When he sees that confident, strong, and independent woman, he sees a reflection of those who raised her. He sees the influence of that parent and the values that have been instilled in that daughter. This woman has standards and boundaries, and she demands respect. A woman who is raised by a loving, attentive, and guiding father has a certain confidence about herself. She knows who she is, and no one can break her self-confidence. When a man is interested in this type of woman, he must approach her correctly or not at all.

Let's take a look at a typical dinner date with a daughter of a king. Her father has exposed her to some of the finer things in life, and he treats her like a lady. She is not easily impressed when some young man shows up with games and tricks. When a man takes a lady to dinner at the local takeout restaurant or diner, she is may be grateful for his company and generosity, but she is not obliged to open the petals of her flower for a meal. She is not easily impressed with a dinner and most certainly does not give up her virtue for a plate of food. This is the woman that expects her date to be on time, courteous, polite and a gentleman. She expects him to pay for dinner and to ensure that she gets home safely. When a woman knows who and whose she is, she operates differently than the rest of the crowd.

While growing up, one of my girlfriends I admired the most was a young lady who was fearless. She was raised in a two-parent home. Both parents were headstrong and liked to call the shots. My friend was closer to her father because he adored her and made her feel special. I was blessed to share in some of those special moments. It was those moments that made me realize what a deep and profound influence a father could have on a daughter. I did not grow up with my father because my parents had divorced when I was very young. By hanging out with my friend, I studied the dynamics of the father-daughter relationship. Sometimes I even noticed my friend's attempt at competing for her father's love, just to tease her mother. I admired my friend because she knew how to get what she wanted from her father so well. As an observer, I saw that she had access to her father's love, money, and attention. When my friend started dating, if the guy lacked in one of those areas, he was quickly dismissed. The first fellow claimed to love her, and he invested lots of money into the relationship, but he did not lavish my friend with his attention. She wanted it all, whereas some other girl would have taken what she could get. She had high standards, and the rest of us ladies respected her for that. She sent a clear message that she was worth something and deserved to have what she wanted. She selected; she did not settle. Many women have a mental picture of the man they desire in their minds however, they settle for less. When you decide to let God select the right man for you, you won't have to settle anymore. You just have to be patient and wait on God.

When a girl grows up in a home where she witnesses her mother being abused by men, she assumes that such behavior is acceptable. I am quite sure that you know at least one woman who is absolutely beautiful inside and out. When this woman enters the room the atmosphere changes. She lights up the room. Her fragrance of love, her calm and cool confidence, and her she-swagger dipped in finesse turns heads. Sometimes this woman is not the most physically attractive woman in the room, or she may not be driving the latest model car, but she is awesome. If she appears confident, it is because she knows the price that she has had to pay to rise and shine each morning. She is a conqueror, an overcomer and she does not need anyone or anything to validate her. She already knows that God has validated her and that makes her feel secure.

If you are wondering why she is still driving that older model car, I respond by saying, it won't be long before a newer model manifests. Just like Cinderella, she may be going through a valley season of life, but I assure you that it won't be long before she rises to the top. Cinderella always comes out on top. She is a true, virtuous woman just like the woman that the Bible so beautifully describes in Proverbs 31. Cinderella knew who she was, and she did not look for love in all the wrong places, but instead desired to be in a place where she would possibly meet her destiny and where her life could change forever. Although the ball was given for the prince, I don't believe she went there necessarily expecting the prince to marry her, to validate her or to make her whole. She was seeking peace from her oppressive environment. She wanted to enjoy life and experience a magical evening. She knew that the prince was destined to appear and ordained to meet his princess. It made perfect sense that Cinderella should have been chosen as the prince's choice. Cinderella had all of the qualities of the virtuous woman. She was thrifty, very diligent, knew what she wanted, and she was kind and compassionate.

We see in the story that she was quite economical. She had planned to wear her old party dress but because she was so busy taking care of everyone she didn't have time to alter it. Surprisingly, her loyal mice friends accessorized that old dress with beautiful remnants of ribbons, bows and sashes. Of course, as soon as the wicked stepmother realized that she had a dress for the occasion, the dress was destroyed. Cinderella was creative and innovative, and she remained a generous and caring lady in spite of where she was in her darkest moment of oppression. She represents what a daughter of royalty should look like.

She did not dress in a manner to entice or seduce the prince. Instead she adorned herself as a lovely stylish lady and she simply wanted to be included in such a beautiful affair. She wanted to feel pretty, be exceptionally beautiful, and be in attendance on that one special night. She had no idea that within 24 hours her life would change forever. As we get to know ourselves better, it helps to know what we need to do, where we need to go, and with whom we need to spend time. We have to know who we are. If we do not know who we are, people will try to define us and shape us into who they would like us to be. Cinderella knew what real love was, because it had been demonstrated by her father. She knew that she was a special person, but she was about to find out what a great woman she really was. We know this because regardless of her situation, she remained kind, gentle, and caring. She knew that her condition was temporary and that soon she would assume her rightful place in the right situation and relationship. Cinderella had the personality traits of a virtuous woman. Her father had once lived in a kingdom, just like God lives in a kingdom and loves his children.

In the Bible, we find a beautiful and captivating story of a young woman who finds love in a peculiar sort of way. She finds love, loses love, and gains a blessed love simply by being an obedient woman of the Lord. In the story of Ruth, we see how a young widow clings to her mother-in-law because they have both lost their husbands. They decide to go back to Naomi's home in Bethlehem. They know that they are strangers in a land where the people serve idols and many gods. Ruth finds herself working on the property of a man who is a relative of her mother-in-law. Immediately he takes notice of Ruth. Boaz instructs his staff to care for her by allowing her to follow behind the collectors of the wheat. He tells his workers not to bother her, but to help her with her work of gleaning. Boaz finds himself studying Ruth while she is going about her business of caring for her mother-in-law. The two women have a special bond and an endearing relationship.

To some, it may seem as though she is wasting her time. Why would she want to hang around an older woman who leads a pretty mundane life? Why is she not trying to find a husband? Doesn't she know that she is getting older each day and that her biological clock is ticking away? Why would she want to work picking up scraps of wheat from what others have dropped? She is doing all of this because she is blessed, inspired, following the guidance of the spirit, and she is highly favored. The blessing is on its way. When God blesses you, you do not need to hunt down a man. God will arrange a divine appointment in the right season. God knows the desires of our hearts, and He will provide the blessing at the right time. Remember that God's ways and thoughts are not like ours, and God uses all things for the good of those who love Him and are called according to His purpose. Ruth did not lean on her own understanding, but she followed her spirit and accepted the insight and wisdom of someone who was wiser than she.

Proverbs 3:5-6 (NKJV) says, "Trust in the Lord with all your heart and lean not on your own understanding; in all your ways acknowledge Him, and He will shall direct your paths." Sometimes we are led to take certain actions that don't make any sense, but we should do it anyway. When God gives you instructions, it is for your own good. Sometimes it doesn't feel good. It may even hurt or make you feel foolish. I assure you that God knows what He is doing. Ruth couldn't explain the condition of her life, and she had no idea what was coming next. She just trusted God, and He prepared a great future for her. God even directed her actions through the counsel of Naomi. Naomi was wise in certain areas of life, and she understood men. Ruth and Naomi had a good relationship; she was respectful and followed Naomi's wise advice. Ruth could have disagreed with Naomi, but she chose to listen and follow her instructions.

It is not uncommon for God to place women in our lives to impart wisdom that will be an asset as we navigate through life. Ruth is a perfect example of a young woman gleaning from the wisdom of a mature woman. Naomi's guidance and coaching changed the course of Ruth's life just as Cinderella's fairy godmother beautifully altered Cinderella's future forever.

One thing that I have learned from reading God's word is that we serve a God of details. When He gives instructions, He tells us precisely what we need to do. Boaz loved Ruth in an extraordinary way, and I say this because he safeguarded her actions and provided for her until she was totally under his care. Ruth would actually be the one who took care of both herself and Naomi as a result of her relationship with Boaz. Boaz was a man of God who had wealth and believed in protecting, providing, and professing his love for the one who had captured his heart.

God arranged a divine appointment for Ruth and Boaz, just as Cinderella encountered one with the prince. Both Ruth and Cinderella were in difficult situations. Cinderella was a slave to her wicked stepmother and stepsisters. Ruth and Naomi were trying to pick up and move on with their lives after a period of grieving and loss. They had to persevere and carry on in spite of what they may have been going through emotionally.

As we closely consider the elements of Ruth's and Cinderella's lives that are parallel, we see that God wants and encourages us to have blessed relationships and sacred unions. Ruth and Boaz's relationship represents a blessed connection and a miracle-laced union. In the earlier stages of their lives Ruth and Cinderella were loved, admired, and respected by the men in their lives. It is important that a woman is taught that a man is supposed to love and respect her from an early age. That first relationship of trust and love should be established by our human father or, 'Daddy' as little girls like to call their fathers. Unfortunately, not everyone who has had a daddy in the home saw a role model of what a real man is supposed to be.

As we study Ruth and Cinderella's journeys, we see that they are strong willed and respectable women. After the death of Ruth's husband, she could have left her mother-in-law, Naomi, and started a new life for herself. Ruth decided to stay with Naomi and travel back to Bethlehem with her. After the death of her father, Cinderella stayed and cared for her wicked stepmother and stepsisters; she did not run away. She worked and cared for them without complaining or being vindictive. Ruth and Cinderella were oppressed by their situations, but they remained positive and did not let their circumstances change their disposition. The common thread that ultimately led to their happy endings was that they chose to remain open to receive love and did not build a wall around their hearts. If you don't learn anything from this story, please know that in times of great difficulty, you must continue to be the same loving person that you truly are. You must also master the virtue of forgiveness by continuing to walk in it. You may have been hurt and in order to protect yourself from enduring emotional pain again, you make the decision to not let a man get close again. The danger in yielding to that type of fear robs you and you alone of the blessings that God may have destined for you to be loved by the right man. If you build a wall around your heart, it blocks love from coming in, and it also blocks love from going out.

These two women simply went about life giving of themselves to others. They were both dedicated to the people in their lives. Family was a major common denominator for these women. God created the institution of family. Cinderella served and cared for her wicked stepsisters and stepmother. Ruth made a commitment to stay with Naomi even though they were heading back to a strange land. They were both loyal and committed to their families. In the beginning of their stories, neither one of these women were looking for love—love found them. Cinderella and Ruth did not know what the future held for them. God connected both women with men of great wealth and of quality; these men wanted to be in long-term relationships. These were men of principle and prominence. Both women experienced the loss of men whom they loved and adored, a father and a husband. Both men were in positions of authority, but they were loving men and catered to these women. If a man of such stature can lovingly impact the life of a young lady, it tells us that there are men who exist who are capable of demonstrating similar qualities.

We see that both women were blessed with people who were assigned to them and they had personalities that were similar to the perfect godmother or mentor. Cinderella was blessed with a fairy godmother, and Ruth had a loving and wise mother-in-law. Both women experienced great oppression, poverty, and hardship. They journeyed to a new place to meet the men of their dreams. Ruth traveled from Moab to Bethlehem. Cinderella traveled to the ball. It seems to me as though the place of destiny may sometimes involve some travel. You have to be in the right place at the right time. Both women worked hard, whether it was in a barley harvest field picking up whatever the harvesters left behind or working all day in a house. Cinderella was transformed into a gorgeously dressed lady who would attended the ball and meet her prince. Ruth was groomed and taught by Naomi how to prepare herself to get Boaz's attention and affection. Ruth exercised self-care, self love, and perfect timing as her keys in attracting love. Cinderella became the princess and moved into the castle, and Ruth married into wealth and security through the wealth of the land. Both Cinderella and Ruth had to take a journey to connect with their future husbands.

These two amazing women learned how to survive in difficult situations while working to reclaim their independence. In the midst of both challenging situations, God turned it around above and beyond anything that they could have ever imagined. They were completely blown away by the goodness of God. Yes, God can bless you abundantly and lavishly.

While penning this story, the Lord inspired me to examine the force and presence of idolatry when desiring a companion or mate. Idolatry is the presence of gods or forces, principalities within, that fight for a place in our hearts. Sometimes, we want money to buy more things and stuff when we should be seeking the love of Jesus and the Word of God. It is good to live comfortably, but it is not okay to love money more than God. Of course, we need money for daily living expenses. Unfortunately, sometimes we use money and things to fill the empty places in our lives and in our souls. Idolatry and the act of seeking things to fill the voids in our lives can possibly lead to hoarding, addiction, and compulsive behavior. We may even self-medicate with things in order to ease the pain that only Jesus can heal. These idols that we focus on, long for, and seek with great passion create a war within us. We want God, but too often we want things more than we want Him. Remember, only

God can fulfill your deepest desire to love and to be loved. God can fill any void that you may have, but you must seek Him.

We spend hours on the phone at night chatting with a girlfriend or boyfriend, but we won't spend fifteen minutes a day reading the Bible. We spend thousands of dollars on things, but we won't tithe.

Sin struggles are evidence of false gods that try to compete with our love for God while consuming our time, leaving God on the back burner instead of in the forefront of our lives. There is this tug and pull that we feel as we make faith-filled choices versus selfish and 'distraction' choices. Some of the gods that we cater to are power, sex, money, shopping, gossip, pleasure, and vanity. The reason why some women may never have a loving relationship is because they believe in the fantasy that a man will solve all of their problems. God did not create man to solve all of our problems, and we must be very careful not to make an idol out of any man. God wants our undivided attention and He does not want to take second place in our lives.

If we seek Him first and delight ourselves in His word both day and night, He will bless us with the desires of our hearts according to His will for our lives. Pray and ask God for the gift of discernment and for His will to be done. No matter what you seek, if it is not in God's will, you will not have it.

For a person who is lonely and tired of spending nights alone, the idea of reading the Bible may seem useless or boring. They may not see the value of spending time with the Creator but, the Bible tells us to seek first the kingdom of God, and all things will be added onto us. I believe that many of us spend years chasing happiness and love in all of the wrong places, only to end up frustrated, broken, and with depleted savings accounts. Trying to fill the void of companionship can be very frustrating.

Let's explore the void. What is the void? The void can be an emptiness of where love should be. A void can be a lack of confidence, self-esteem, or a feeling of being unattractive. Sometimes it is the void of a parent's love. Lack of self-care can also create a void because you can reach a point of emptiness, exhaustion, and depression. We know that lack of affection, touch, and feeling appreciated or cared for can also create a void. Oh, how we try to fill that void with shopping, relationships, gossip, busyness, self-criticism, exercising, stuff, and sex. We go from one filler to the next, and all the time that little voice is asking us to spend time being still. That still small voice is calling us into the presence of God so that He may minister to us, love us, inspire us, heal us, and guide us. We go on searching and traveling, trying to find what is tugging at our hearts. We need to seek God, seek Jesus, and allow the Holy Spirit to comfort us.

So, what do you do while waiting for your prince? Well, by now, you realize that waiting for your prince takes a lot of patience. One thing is for sure, you should not go about looking for the prince but allow the prince to find you. You should be focusing on God and seeking Jesus so that your heart is positioned to receive what God is preparing for you. Do not go hunting for the prince, but make yourself available by being social, interesting and appealing. Educate yourself, care for your temple, enjoy traveling, and maintain a healthy lifestyle. Work on healing and improving your self-worth and value. If you really knew who you were and how much God loves you, you wouldn't waste any time chasing anyone or tolerating half the foolishness that you do now. It is time to stop approaching your desire to be loved in the manner in which the world is encouraging you to do. When you dress up in alluring and provocative ways to get a man's attention, you will get it, but it won't be from the type of man you really want. If you want a man to treat you like the lady that Cinderella represents, then you should demonstrate that you have the qualities that she possessed. If you can be honest with yourself and recognize that you don't have those qualities, then I suggest that you start working on yourself so that you will stand out like Cinderella did in the midst of a room full of other females.

Address your issues. Yes, we all have some issues. It usually starts during the time of childhood and while we are still in the crib. Maybe your family was normal, and your parents had the perfect marriage or had a great relationship even though they were not married. However, the majority of us had some level of dysfunction in our lives as we grew up. At some point, if you do not address those issues, they will show up in your present relationship. If you have been holding a grudge against men since you were a little girl, then it will at some point surface in your future relationships.

You are a product of your experiences, environment, method of communication, and relationship with God and man. This is what shaped you into the woman or man that you are now. If you experienced your parents' relationship as loving, caring, and with total commitment, then you understand why you may want to stay married forever. If you saw them fussing and fighting often, or your mother crying and miserable most days, you might think that arguing constantly is a part of marriage. Of course couples argue, but there is such a thing as fighting fair. If you do not understand how most men communicate in relationships, you might be offended most days. We bring our vulnerabilities and insecurities into our relationships. We can only maintain a pseudo relationship for so long, and then our true selves appear. Just as the pretend prince is eventually found out, so is the wannabe princess. The truth always comes out, and what is in the dark eventually comes to the light.

Very often women marry the wrong men. If you find yourself in such a situation, you must trust God to see you through that relationship. Remember, you formed a covenant by declaring a scared promise so you both need to do the relationship work. You cannot make a relationship work by yourself. As soon as you realize that you married the wrong one, the first thing that you should do is pray for guidance and then forgive yourself. Forgive yourself for your frustration and your reaction to the current situation. Ask God to prepare you for what is about to occur in the days up ahead. Sometimes when the marriage is not going in the right direction, people tend to beat themselves up and complain. Self-blame serves no purpose. More than likely, you chose the frog and not God. It is unfair but often God gets blamed for the poor choices that we make. Why do women choose the wrong husbands? Sometimes we are trying to beat that biological clock, and we feel that we must get married as soon as possible. Those types of rushed marriages seem to have a greater failure rate. Sometimes we are simply lonely. We cannot stand spending any more nights alone staring at the ceiling and wishing someone was there. In some instances, we honestly thought that they were princes even though we saw the warning signs, like the overindulgence of alcohol, the too-frequent gambling games, being quick to anger, and the roaming eyes. Let us also not forget that women sometimes choose to ignore what is obvious because they would rather have a man than no man at all.

It's so sad to hear some of the stories that women tell themselves. A friend recently shared with me how she told her husband that she had absolutely nothing more to give him. She had given all that she could of herself. She admitted to him that he took everything away from her, including her money, joy, peace, happiness, and an opportunity to have children. She went on the say how he used her, and he is still disrespecting her by allowing his family to have access to their money through the use of a credit card that they will never pay back. She sat there with me and played victim for fifteen minutes. Finally, I suggest that she take responsibility for the part that she played in the madness. She became silent. There we sat for a few minutes as the truth filled the air.

As I listen to the news and hear stories of what is going on in the world, I've come to realize that women are under some sort of spiritual attack. I always say if you want to understand the end, then study the beginning. Since the beginning of time in the Garden of Eden, it seems as though women have been paying a high price to maintain their power. Women are a gift to the world from God. God loves women, and He understands the heart of a woman. God blessed Adam with Eve. As we hear more and more stories about how women and children are abused and mistreated throughout the world, it makes one wonder why. Eve was distracted by the enemy, and her decision to eat the forbidden fruit and share it with Adam changed the course of the world forever. On we go, living life as romance, sex, money, and power vie for our allegiance in today's society each and every way every day. So, what is the solution? When the Lord God takes His rightful place on the throne of our hearts, we will have victory. God must always come first no matter what.

When we first start out in life looking for the prince, we move forward excitedly with all of our hopes and dreams. We dress a certain way and we act a certain way. We are stylish and confident as we socialize while stepping out for those evening or afternoon affairs. We strive to put our best foot forward as we seek the one who will make our dreams come true. Sadly, many women do not have a clear definition of what a prince looks like or should be. Many women deceive themselves into believing they can change a man. Please understand, God is the only one who can change anyone from who they have become to who they should be.

We show up to dinner as vulnerable as can be wishing that he is the one. We often sit there and share exactly what is on our minds; we describe to this stranger exactly who we want him to be. Yes, we tell the stranger how the prince should look, behave and operate. At the same time, this façade of a prince is sitting there becoming an image of a prince in her mind. He now has enough knowledge to pretend to be everything that she ever wanted in a man. He has the perfect blueprint to represent her heart's desire as her prince. He puts on his best behavior and acts like a prince until he has won her heart. Then she finds herself self not in the palace but in a pit or a mess.

Okay, let's get real. The reason why so many women find themselves in the pit is because they are not positioned to receive a prince. While waiting for your prince, please consider the following practices and thoughts:

1. Seek God and His kingdom, and all good things will be added unto you.

2. If you did not grow up with your father or any positive strong male role model in your life, please find one and study him.
3. It is important that you deal with your baggage. Your baggage is all of the hurts, disappointments, and setbacks that you are still holding on to in your mind. You can fix your mind if you ask God to heal your heart.
4. You must learn how to make yourself happy with or without a man. This is very important because a true prince is more likely to be attracted to a happy and confident princess rather than to one who is miserable and waiting for him to make her happy.
5. Work on becoming the best princess that you can possibly be. Practice and visualize that you are already in a wonderful, loving and healthy relationship.
6. Your mind and heart should be in the position to receive a prince. Get yourself together. Purge and delete what and who needs to be released, in order for you to have peace and attract love into your life.
7. Be thrifty and wise with money as the virtuous woman. Save some, spend some and be generous with some.
8. Walk with the godly and seek counsel of those who love the Lord. Your inner circle is very important to your growth and advancement socially, spiritually and intellectually.
9. Enjoy your life. Have fun and celebrate yourself daily. Every day is a great day to eat from your fine china and sip from your crystal glasses.
10. Praise, worship, and thank God for what He is about to do!

11. Act as though you are already living in the palace and have your prince.
12. Serve those in your life with love, compassion, and kindness.
13. Forgive those who have hurt you, and receive your own forgiveness from God. Yes, forgive yourself for not always selecting but for settling for less than what you know that you deserve.

There were times when Cinderella was frustrated, simply because she was an amazing and wonderful person. She always had the best of intentions; she was kind, respectful, generous, and caring. She was cautious not to hurt, disrespect, or abuse anyone. She often wondered how long she would remain in her situation, and whether anyone out there even cared about her. When guests visited the family, they never included her in their conversations or even noticed her. They just needed her to cater to their needs like bringing them something to eat or resting their hats and coats. She wanted someone to visit her too. She also wanted to be free to go and come as she pleased, to enjoy the simple liberty of freedom and independence.

Cinderella was in a difficult, oppressive place, but she overcame. It says in Philippians 4:13 (NKJV), "I can do all things through Christ who strengthens me." God knows how to make your enemies your footstool, and He can provide opportunities for you to bless your friends. God can also use your enemies to bless you. No weapons formed against you shall prosper. If you are in a challenging situation it is best to remain peaceful while maintaining a good attitude so that you may not block your blessings. The key is to keep the movement of love flowing in and out of our hearts. So many times, women are so affected by past hurts that they put up walls to block out any future hurt. But remember, a wall is a wall; nothing can get in, and nothing can get out. God will often use people like the stepmother and stepsisters to challenge us right before He blesses us.

Everyone has encountered people like the mean stepmother and stepsisters at one point. I am here to tell you that what the devil meant for evil can be turned around for your good in an instance. This is the challenge of this secret: we must continue to allow love to flow in and out of our hearts. Of course, as we forgive others, we must also learn to love some people from a distance.

The main reason why you may have gone crazy, seeking a prince without scrutinizing the situation, is because of the next ten letters: The Wedding!

On the glorious morning that God woke me up and prompted me to write this book, the first image I saw was Kate Middleton and Prince William. There they were in a horse-drawn carriage with majestic, galloping white horses escorted by uniformed horsemen and trumpets blaring. It was so majestic and so regal, and I was overwhelmed with unexplainable emotion and happiness. My eyes filled with tears of joy. I was so excited and happy for Kate. She was living the dream that millions of women around the world sought after and hungered for. I remember that the television commentators frequently referred to her as a commoner, and I thought to myself, that means that there is hope for all of the other little girls out there who still believe in the dream and the magic. As I enjoyed the ceremony and the all of the fabulous energy surrounding the occasion, I saw God's signature on that moment in time. I concluded that God's children are heirs to His Kingdom. Children of God are of true kingdom royalty and they are blessed. The British Royal family is stately and honorable, but so are you who accept Jesus as your Lord and Savior. You are members of a heavenly and spiritual family. So as we consider the drive and the tenacity in which women seek to secure a prince for that special day and sometimes driven to near insanity, possible bankruptcy, please understand, it is all for them to have the fairytale wedding of their dreams.

In this day and age, it is not unusual for a bride to spend over $50,000 for her wedding. You are probably asking yourself what would possess someone to invest that amount of money in a one-day event. The answer is very simple; she will be the princess of the day, and it will be her day! She and millions of women, including me, have dreamed about our wedding day since we were little girls. We go to weddings, we are flower girls, we are bridesmaids, and we can't get enough of it. We vow that one day we will be the princess and it will be a glorious day!

The amount of stress, aggravation, and resentment that can manifest during the wedding planning stages is sad, yet comical at times. For some, the wedding is the most important thing to which they have ever totally committed themselves. Now, I am not speaking about the marriage. Statistics show that 50 percent of the marriages in the United States now end in divorce. So why are we focusing more on the wedding and not looking closer at who we are marrying? It appears as though some women would rather have a jerk for a husband than no husband at all.

The story of Cinderella has influenced the lives of millions of women. It has afforded many undeserving men a shot at marriage. That's right, I said it: millions of women have married people with whom they had no right entering into a covenant.

Millions of women have married men who are not even an image of a prince. Millions of women have spent millions of dollars on fairytale weddings that did not last two years, and it was all for less than happily ever after. Cinderella's story has changed the world. Tonight, hundreds of little girls will hear this story for the first time, and the seed will be planted in their minds for a lifetime and eventually take root in their hearts that they must find a prince. The wedding and event planning business should thank Cinderella for the billions of dollars that her life on paper has fueled for their business. Millions of men should thank God for the virtuous women who have blessed their lives and taught them how to love and care for a family. Some men should thank God because they know that they were never a prince, but yet they were blessed with one of God's beautiful, sacred princesses.

The lovely and romantic bedtime story of Cinderella has changed the way millions of women and men view love. This sweet and beautiful story filled with its ups and downs and glorious ending is impacting how we approach romance. In the middle of this story of magic and happy ending, God inspires us. Of course, we know that Jesus is the everlasting beloved Prince but, God still has prepared princes for His daughters on earth. I am suggesting that if you look closely you will see God in the miracle of this story and our lives. God has inspired me to pen this story and has whispered in my ears for years that Jesus is the prince. Every young woman who cannot find a prince, has divorced the prince, or wants a prince can find him in Jesus Christ. It is true that some women will never marry, but they are not alone. Some women will even settle for someone else's prince, knowing that it is not right. She will allow herself to be his second choice or to be a side chick. In the next few weeks someone will spend over one hundred thousand dollars on a wedding to impress people who don't care about them. Why would someone spend her last savings on a wedding that she is not sure will last? Why would someone marry a person that did not love her? Why would someone marry a man who is seeking to gain citizenship of a country through marriage? She would do it just to have a man. She would do it simply to be Cinderella for one day and to drive off in that limousine to happily ever after.

What is happily ever after? It is unattainable through worldly means but, with Jesus in your life, the happily ever after is available. If you have a relationship with Jesus, you can have peace that the world does not understand and cannot take away. You can have peace, even in the midst of a storm. We all know that, no marriage is perfect and that not all marriages are made in heaven. Christians get married and divorced all the time. Marriages are challenging and take work. You learn how to compromise and check your ego when you are in a real, committed relationship known as marriage. There is no "I" in marriage land; it is all about two people. If you add children to the equation, the relationship takes a more complicated turn. Marriages are a blessing, and they are ordained by God. God is the creator of this concept and he has defined marriage as a union between a man and a woman.

Cinderella has changed the course of our economy with the astronomical amounts of money that is annually poured into the wedding & event planning business. Weddings have taken on a whole new trend in our country. Can you imagine brides planning very extravagant weddings yet, not having a clear vision of where they will live? Most men do not want to deal with the wedding shenanigans. They simply want to get married and settle in someplace quiet and romantic. The story of Cinderella has surely impacted the lives of men over the years. Some men do not want to be put on display and spend money on a one day affair when they know that they do not even have the down payment for a home.

Glass Slipper Affirmation: I am a princess of the Kingdom of God. I will not minimize who I am for anyone or anything. I am beautiful, talented, whole, and I am wonderfully made by the Creator. I am blessed with life, and God wants me to have it more abundantly. The man who God has chosen for me is on his way to me now.

chapter 2

The Strengthened Princess

I can do all things through Christ who strengthens me.

—Philippians 4:13 (NKJV)

Secret #2: God will give you the strength to persevere, complete the assignment and have the victory.

We must admit that as the story progressed, Cinderella found herself in a difficult place. She was oppressed and abused emotionally and physically, but she overcame. She rose above the ordinary through divine intervention. Her daily mantra was probably found in Philippians 4:13 (NKJV), which says, "I can do all things through Christ who strengthens me." This scripture would have given her the strength and fortitude to do her work each day while maintaining a positive attitude. If given the opportunity, she would have clung to the word of God, and eventually He would have turned her enemies into her footstool.

God can use your enemies and that oppressive situation to bless you beyond your wildest dreams. Enemies can serve a purpose and play a major role that leads to your greatest moment of happiness. While enemies are working, God is working too. He will send a friend, an inspirational message, or a praise song, to bless you in a special way that could have only been His work. He will always send someone who can be a comfort. Before Jesus left us on earth, He promised to send the Holy Spirit to comfort and dwell in us as we travel along this journey of life. We have the Holy Spirit, and we have angels on earth who are called friends. It is indeed a blessing to have a good and true friend. In the story, we see that Cinderella had many friends, and they loved her too. They filled the hollowness in her life. The old horse, mice, and dog loved Cinderella because she was kind, she was nice, and cared for them. She treated them with love and communicated with them all the time.

Everyone needs at least one good trusted friend. We need someone who will stand with us through thick and thin. A friend is one who will walk with you when everyone else has left the scene. A true friend can be trusted with your secrets, doesn't judge you, will encourage you as you move through life, and most important will be honest with you. There are times when we all need to hear the truth. Sometimes we need to hear the truth from a true friend. A friend will push you toward your dreams and will support and encourage you when you don't have the strength to move forward. True friends will defend your name and believe in you when you do not believe in yourself. A special friend is one whom you can call at three in the morning and say, "I need to talk." A friend will make you dinner and bring it over when you aren't feeling well. She or he can listen to your heart, and you can share what is on your mind. She understands you. She will call you after the party to make sure that you got home safe and that you are okay.

The three main characteristics that true friends display are caring, being trustworthy, and committed to the friendship. They will not play games with your heart and emotions. They may know what pushes your buttons, but they won't push them. They genuinely want to see you happy and enjoying life. They are happy for you when you are doing well, and they will support you when you need to be uplifted. There's nothing like having a friend to celebrate the good times with you, as well as hold your hand through the tough times. Friends can cry with you as well as laugh with you. Sometimes they can look at you and immediately know what you are feeling. They even know when to give you space and your private time to work through your thoughts and emotions.

We clearly see Cinderella's kindness as she interacted with the stepfamily's mean cat. Ironically, his name was Lucifer. God loves us and created us to fellowship with Him. We should not ever feel that we cannot seek God in the time of trouble. He did not intend for us to ever feel lonely or live an isolated life. In the story, God provided Cinderella with pets who loved her and who would be there for her when He finally turned that situation around. He would use them to fulfill the night of purpose and destiny. On that faithful night, the mice would turn into horses. The old horse turned into a coachman, and the dog became a footman. These are the gifts of love that the Lord place around Cinderella.

At one time or another, there is a person or a group of people who made all of the difference in our lives. Perhaps it was a grandmother, an aunt, or a friend of the family who poured love into us when we were growing up. Maybe it was a co-worker who stood by us when no one else cared or could be honest with us. I remember when I going through a tough time, a lady named Isabella gave me a beautiful, easy-to-read Bible. Now, I have had many Bibles. Some of my Bibles are very expensive and have beautiful illustrations, but I always like to keep Isabella's Bible, as well as the one that my dear Grandmother gave me. Everyone needs a friend, and God always sends someone to walk alongside of us. We also know that even when we cannot see anyone there, Jesus is walking with us. The Bible tells us that God will never leave us or forsake us. We can be assured of that. So the next time that you are overwhelmed or burdened, go to God and pour your heart out to Him. Tell Him exactly what is on your mind and heart. Allow God to comfort and strengthen you.

We must also remember to be kind to everyone as we move along in life because we never know who is there on assignment from the Lord. We never know who a person really is or who they know that could be a helping hand in the future. So many times, we have seen where a person of power mistreats another, and then the table of organization turns in favor of the other. Of course, we would like to know that when the table turns, the victim does not retaliate but will forgive and move on. We are all human, and forgiveness is the turning point in any relationship where a person has been hurt, disappointed, or taken advantage of.

One of the greatest lessons of this story is that of forgiveness. Cinderella eventually succeeds in life. She was able to leave the wicked family members behind and enter into a new life of happiness without seeking revenge. If you have enemies or know of those who mean you harm, keep praying for them and meditate on this scripture daily, "No weapon formed against you shall prosper, and every tongue which rises against you in judgment you shall condemn." Isaiah 54:17 (NKJV). Remain in peace and keep a good attitude so you do not block your blessings. The key is to keep the movement of love flowing in and out of our lives. So many times, when we are offended by past hurts, we put up a wall to block out any future hurt. But remember that a wall is a wall, and nothing can get in or out.

    If Cinderella was a modern day woman of God, on the morning of the ball she would have probably spent some time in prayer. After all, Cinderella was accustomed to rising early in the morning in order to get her more physically demanding chores completed before the afternoon sun reached its apex. Cinderella was a loner, and she kept to herself. She wasn't one to run all over town and share her story of oppression and misfortune. She carried her cross. She pondered on the things that her father shared with her in secret. She knew who she was, and she knew that there was something very special about her. She was strong and faithful, and she believed that a better day was coming. She knew that one day, the sun would come out again. If you are discouraged about life and love right now, simply hold on and keep the faith. Wait on the Lord. God is aware of every teardrop and every care that keeps you up at night. I believe that God is going to deliver you from the darkness and bring you into the glorious light. The situation that you are in is temporary. Have faith and know that God is with you.

    I think the modern day Cinderella would have prayed like this:

    Dear Father in heaven, I love you and adore you. Thank You for this new day. Thank You for Your blessings in my life. I know that you have a better life in store for me, and I am waiting patiently on you. I am a good girl, Father, and I am obedient and thankful for what I have, but I would like to have my own family. I want a companion, a husband that you will chose for me. I do not want to choose my husband, Father. I want you to send the right God-fearing and loving man to me. Since I was a child, all that I have ever wanted was to love and be loved. I know that you are a jealous God, Father, and that I should not put anyone before you, but I am asking you for a good husband Lord in the name of Jesus.

Your word says that I should seek you first, and then you will add many good things onto me. I am waiting patiently, Lord, because I know that it is all in your time and not mine. I am thankful for my dear animal friends, their companionship, and the fun that we have together. I know that when I finally arrive at a place of great blessings, I will not forget them. Thank You for sending them to care for me and look out for my safety. When I am blessed, I will surely bless them.

Lord, please continue to bless me with knowledge, wisdom and understanding. I still do not understand why my stepmother and stepsisters dislike like me so. What makes a woman dislike another woman who has never harmed her or spoken against her? Shouldn't women love and support each other? It seems as though men respect each other enough to have certain man codes or principles in place. My stepsisters should be bonding with me. We should be living in peace and enjoying the fruits of this land.

Family members have disagreements all the time, but there seems to be a root of bitterness and evil here. If the prince of the land is going to have a grand ball, why can't we all go? I don't need the most beautiful gown; I just want to go. I want to sing and dance and see the prince dance with the other pretty ladies there. I will even help my stepsisters prepare for the gala. Not only can I help everyone get dressed, I can apply makeup and style their hair to the style of their liking. I simply want to be included in the fun. Why do women play that silly game of exclusion and rejection, ignoring those whom they dislike for no reason? It hurts and it divides us. Men stick together, so why can't we?

Lord, in spite of it all, I still love my stepmother and my stepsisters. I may not like what they do to others, but I love them and forgive them for their wicked ways. I have cooked, clean, ironed, ran errands, and listened to their complaints and whining. I am doing the best that I can. I do not condone their behavior, so I love them from a distant place. I have a wish in my heart, though. Can you please bless me so that I will one day find true love wrapped in dreamy romance? May I also be able to live apart from my stepfamily and maybe care for them from a distance? Lord, you know that it takes finances to do your work and care for others, so please bless my vision with your provision. I do not want to be surrounded by this toxic and negative energy anymore. I am not perfect, Lord, and I confess my sins to you and ask you to please forgive me if I have sinned against you in any way. I accept your forgiveness, dear Lord. I love you, dear Father, and I worship you.

Well, I must complete my chores and help the stepfamily prepare for the ball this evening. Father, you know my heart. I wish to attend the ball. Lord, if you choose to bless one of my stepsisters or whomever the blessed one is to catch the prince's eyes, then I pray that He will love her forever, and they will live happily ever after. Thank You in advance for answering this prayer, Father. I declare that I can do all things through Christ who strengthens me. With love, Cinderella.

The key to this secret is that even though the race of life is sometimes overwhelming, God will see us through. Did you know that God can put His super on your natural? There are days that are very difficult to complete, yet God will give you the endurance, strength, and courage to carry you through the day. You will wonder, "How in the world did I do it today?" God can heal the pain, remove the spirit of offense, and put a song in your heart. It is true that negative situations can sap you of your strength and energy, but God can infuse you with His joy. You can work and get your college degree at night. You can be a great single parent and get that promotion at work. Tap into the power of God's word and allow Him to replace that spirit of exhaustion with His rest.

When your world is spinning out of control, be still. Find a quiet spot and spend time with the Lord. In spite of all that is going on, you must also remember to never allow anyone to change the beautiful person that you are. If we allow others to infect us with negativity, then they have won the battle of spreading evil. So many people in this world have been hurt and abused, yet they have chosen to live their lives as loving, caring, and generous people. These acts of kindness and humility are what actually heals a broken heart and lifts the spirit. The Bible shows that Jesus had a special love for the brokenhearted and those who suffered and were oppressed.

The challenge of this secret is to forgive and move on with your life. The forgiveness is for you, not the abuser. Also, forgiving someone does not mean that you condone their behavior. Forgiving others means that you will no longer give them the power to deposit anger and bitterness in your life. In the case of family, we sometimes have to love some relatives from a distance. I know that you cannot stop loving some people, so it is best to keep your distance from those who try to spitefully use, abuse, and hurt you. We must continue to allow love to flow in, through, and out of our hearts.

If someone has hurt you, then you must pray and ask God to heal you of any anger and bitterness. If you don't they may settle in your heart and deep roots can start to grow. You know that hurting people hurt other people. No one can determine how long it will take to heal from the wounds inflicted upon them. It's usually a process, not something attained overnight. Some people are able to move along quicker than others from pain and mistreatment. The key to healing is to ask God to heal your brokenness. Only God can heal a broken heart or spirit. Intensify your love for self and nurture yourself just as you do for everyone else. Turn your love of self up to an intense level. Care for yourself and even forgive yourself for those feelings of anger and disappointment.

In the garden of Gethsemane, Jesus certainly felt the heaviness of what it was like to be alone as a human. This is probably the way that Cinderella felt in that garden just before her fairy godmother appeared. She had done all that she could do to please those around her. She was kind and caring, and yet they mistreated her. There was nothing that she could do to gain their love; they did not like her, and that was that. She didn't think that there was any hope of her attending the ball. Nothing about her situation said that it would have a happy ending. She was now at a point of total surrender. That's what it takes for us as well, to let go and let God so that He can change our situation. She was on the verge of a total breakthrough, but she didn't know it. It was coming, and she was about to be delivered from the oppression she was living. Her deliverance came in three days. The day that the invitation arrived was one of excitement and expectation, and then the day of preparation was the worst after the stepsisters destroyed her dress. The day of glory, however was one when the prince would appear at her doorstep with her other glass slipper in his hand and claim her as his future princess! This event took place right in front of those who were against her, and her success was the greatest payback that anyone could ever imagine. It was as though God Himself had fought her battle. He did what she could not have done for herself.

Sometimes it takes wisdom to realize that the battle is not ours, but that it is the Lord's. We have to ask for wisdom to recognize what we can do and what we need God to do. Pray for God to put His super on your natural. Rest in the peace of God and have confidence that He will deliver you from the hands of your enemies. Remain loving and kind and in peace.

Now, let's examine the choice of forgiveness. First of all, forgiveness is for the one who was hurt or offended. When we forgive others, we set ourselves free. Is it easy? No, it is not, but there is one known as the Holy Spirit who can guide us through the forgiveness process. When you forgive, you are not surrendering to the pain or to the abuser. Of course, your ego wants you to think that you are weak. When you forgive, you have the courage of a hero who has decided to move on with his or her life. God's word says, "Vengeance is mine says the Lord." It would be arrogant of us to think that we can repay evil for evil when that punishment is not ours to render. Forgiving is not an admission that we are weak or that we gave up. The forgiver releases the power and control that the offense or pain has caused. It is saying, "I choose to get on with my life and let this go." For us Christians, it is a declaration that we have turned the situation over to God. It is His battle, not ours. It is the liberation of our minds and spirits as well as taking our lives back.

The forgiver benefits, of course, but as we forgive others, we must learn to take certain actions. Once we forgive a person, we can make some of the following choices.

1. Love some people from a distance. This often works well with some family members.
2. Cease having any contact with the offender.
3. Take back control of your happiness. Allow yourself to be happy again. No one can make you happy. You are responsible for your own happiness.
4. Do not allow anyone to determine your level of success or accomplishment.
5. Know when to let go and let God. Trust God with your future and believe that His plan is the best for your life.
6. In every experience there are lessons to be learned. Learn the lesson well so that it may not be repeated.
7. Rid yourself of any guilt associated with the incident.

Another great lesson in this story is when Cinderella was blessed and put into a position where she could have threatened the stepfamily that she would repay them for tormenting her, she did not. She was not spiteful or revengeful. She would have done what we are supposed to do and that is to let God fight our battles for us. She remained a person of great integrity, character, and humility. She stood her ground and did not allow the situation to get into her spirit. She had done all that she could, so she just stood like the Bible tells us to do. So even though you may have been hurt in the past, continue to work on yourself and become a better partner for your future mate. Develop yourself so that you can bring some valuable and meaningful contributions to the relationship. Work on being whole; stay positive and get ready for a new relationship. You may have baggage, but so does your prince. We all have baggage, but every day, people turn their situations around for the better. Let's take the lemons we've collected over time and make some sweet lemonade.

As our princess was getting ready to attend the ball, it reminded me of the night that Esther went to be with the king. In the scriptures, it states that Esther was given an opportunity to spend one intimate night with the king. The king was unaware that he was oppressing her people. By pleasing the king, Esther was able to save her people from being destroyed. She planned and prepared for that special night, when she would have one opportunity to be with the king and persuade him to save her people. Of course, Esther was on a mission whereas Cinderella was simply swept up in the magic of the evening, but they both made an impact on the heart of a man who would change the course of their worlds.

Oh, how we so often long for the opportunity to meet or be in the company of that special someone. We visualize and fantasize about what we would do if we met or connected with that person. We think about all the things we would say. Cinderella had one chance to get it right, and she maximized the moment by giving the prince her undivided attention. Of course, we all know that she captured his eye when she entered the ballroom. As the evening progressed, she looked directly into his eyes and allowed him to see who she really was. It was in her eyes that he saw how beautiful, forgiving, loving, and caring she was. He saw hope of a bright future in her eyes and he felt that her intentions were pure. He saw that she was bright and intelligent. He saw that she was lovely and would make the best possible queen in the future. He was probably overwhelmed that evening, and did not expect to find a princess candidate for his future. Cinderella made quite an impression on him even though all of the available women in the town were at the ball. He may have imagined she could be a world leader and possibly the mother of his children because she was patient and kind. As he gazed into her eyes they also revealed her pain and disappointment and he could hear it in her voice. She had been taken advantage of, but she was not bitter or angry. She was not like the other young ladies who stood off to the side, rolling their eyes and continuing to display bad attitudes. He saw a young woman who had seen more than her share of sadness and disappointment. She fascinated him, and he couldn't wait to see her again. He wanted to know more about her. She was free spirited and beautiful inside and out. He imaged taking long walks and enjoying horseback riding trips with her. He knew that his father would be so pleased with his decision to select this beautiful young woman. Where did she live? Who were her people? How would she feel about being married in a matter of days and living the rest of her life as royalty? It seemed as though she fit in and would be loved by all of the palace staff. After all, she was moving from a place of being unwelcomed to a place where she would be welcomed, respected, and cared for.

Once the stepsisters left for the night, she thought it was all over for her. She was sad and found her way to the garden, where she poured out her heart hoping her cry would reach heaven. She couldn't help but think her chance to meet the prince was over. A smile appeared when she imagined what it would be like to dance with a real prince. Would he kiss her hand? Would he twirl her around and then draw her close to him? What a great feeling that must be, to be held in the arms of a prince who was about to choose the woman of his dreams. She knew that it would be a very exciting night, but she would not be there. The stepsisters had already convinced her that she would help them prepare for the ball, but she would have to stay home. Well, as you know, your enemies may try to intrude, but God has the final say in the matter of your future. While they were planning her night, good things were being planned for her too. Behind the scenes an auspicious evening was being planned.

At first she was shy when he approached her and asked her for a dance. She wanted to dance so badly, but her nerves were on edge. Then calmness came over her. She took a breath and stepped out onto that shiny dance floor. So many eyes were on her but, she looked away and kept her eyes on the prince the entire time. During the first dance, it was a little quiet. Then he pulled her closer as the other ladies looked on in great anticipation. They wanted to know how much longer they would have to wait for a dance or even capture his glance. He couldn't see or hear anything or anyone else except Cinderella. He was totally captivated with her beauty, and her fragrance surrounded them. It was a fragrance of love and intoxication and alluring passion. Their hearts synchronized and beat as one. A feeling of deep warmth and comfort surrounded them. They both knew that they were starting something that would never end.

In Matthew 26:36–46, Jesus is in the garden of Gethsemane. In the Bible, blessings are found in many gardens over a period of time. The life of man and woman began in the Garden of Eden. Something magnificent happens in the garden. We all have a garden, but we must ensure that the garden is someplace that invites Jesus. After the resurrection, Jesus did not have to be concerned about going down into darkness anymore. If you are in darkness, Jesus can call you into the light just like he did with Lazarus. Jesus loves us, and He will even send someone into a dark place to get us out. We carry the light of Jesus because He lives in us. We are the light that shines forth in this dark world. We are the spiritual ambassadors on the job and in the earth. We harvest the fruits of the spirit, as it says in Galatians 5:22 (NKJV), "But the fruit of the Spirit is love, joy, peace, longsuffering, kindness, goodness, faithfulness, gentleness, self-control. Against such there is no law."

In the Bible, we find the story of David, who went from the field caring for the animals to the kingdom. David was the youngest son of Jesse, who was a sheepherder. Israel's first king was King Saul. Because King Saul was disobedient, the prophet Samuel was inspired to seek out the next king of Israel. In the meantime, things were unstable in Israel, with fighting between the Israelites and the Philistines. All the while, God was preparing the next young man who would be king. God instructed Samuel to visit Jesse because one of his sons would be the next king. Jesse presented all of his sons to Samuel, except David who was out in the field taking care of the sheep. When Samuel met David, he anointed him with oil and blessed him.

In the interim, war continued in Israel. A giant by the name of Goliath continued to terrify the people of Israel for a period of forty days and forty nights. One day when David took food to the soldiers and his brothers, who were out on the battlefield, David saw the giant, and he decided to fight the giant with five stones. With one stone, David knocked the giant to the ground, and then he cut off his head. God gave David the victory! Saul made David the leader of his army. During David's tenure as head of the army, he had many victories, and the people of Israel loved him.

As the story continues, King Saul and his three sons perished in one of the battles. David became the king of Israel! Unfortunately, David sinned with Bathsheba, and he had her husband killed in battle. David married Bathsheba, and they had a son named Solomon, who was the wisest king that Israel has ever had.

So we see that it is not unusual that God can elevate a person from hard, back-breaking work to the luxuries of a palace and kingdom living. It is not unusual that God always has a plan for us and a great future for us as written in Jeremiah 29:11.

Now, let's take a look at those stepsisters and their mother. They were a hot mess! You may recognize them immediately. We all know at least one person like the stepsisters. They were jealous, trifling, and deceitful. Thank God that the Lord usually uses their type in our lives to propel us to higher blessings. Interestingly enough, they are necessary for our success and greatest blessing. They are simply a test, and they can be used to propel us to the next level of greatness. We find them along the journey of our lives, in our families, on the job, and in the church. Some are friends with ill intentions. In any event, if we follow God's word and pray for our enemies, He will use them to bless us. We will come out from under their oppressive hands better, wiser, and stronger. If you ever get to a point where you do not understand why you encounter many individuals who have hidden agendas and try to oppose you, give thanks because you are truly blessed. Throughout the Bible, we see that all great men and women rose from dark situations. Sometimes, there was a Judas in the midst of it all.

A few years ago, while experiencing a season of loss, I was reminded that God has the final say in all situations and challenging times, even in the middle of the storms of life. During a storm many things can happen. You can lose everything in the middle of a storm and look as though you do not have a care in the world. God can preserve the way you look. As my pastor sometimes says, "Thank God that we don't look like what we have been through!" God can preserve your appearance and keep you in His perfect peace. During that time of loss, a sermon I heard reminded me that if God brought me to it, He would bring me through it. Now, let's be clear: God is a good and loving God, but if it is happening, God allowed it. Of course God wishes His children to be blessed, blossom, and flourish. The word tells us that He wants our souls to prosper. There are even times when God will allow the enemy to challenge us in order to push us to the next level. Dealing with the enemy is uncomfortable and requires a closer walk with Jesus. Haven't you notice that we always run to God when times are the toughest? Well, that's a good thing. Of course, it is better when you have a long-standing relationship with our Father in heaven. When we spend time with God daily, we can hear Him when He speaks to us, especially during our times of trouble. Yes, sometimes the oppressor serves a godly purpose, and that is to help you fulfill your purpose.

Hopefully by this stage, you have identified what your purpose is in life. If you don't know what it is, then go to God and ask Him to reveal it to you. Spend time with God, talk to Him as you would a dear friend, or address Him as He simply is, your Father in heaven. Take notice of what your best talents and skills are. What do you do that is effortless and brings you enjoyment and happiness? What is it that you are passionate about? Finding your passion can be a wonderful adventure.

Once God reveals to you what your purpose is, start moving in that direction. Start the new business, go back to school, or do whatever it takes to fulfill the purpose of your life. Interestingly, as soon as you start investing time and energy into your purpose, things will start to happen. All of a sudden, you may encounter unnecessary drama and distractions. Beware of the distractions that are coming from those closest to you. You must remain focus and be mindful of your time and resources. Use your resources to build up your business, project, or ministry. The main reason why some people may not like you for any apparent reason, or try to make your life miserable, is because they recognize that you are special. You have gifts and talents in you that the enemy is trying to steal, kill, or destroy. It is during this time that you must pay attention to who has access to you because the enemy also creates chaos, confusion and creates atmospheres of deception. Most importantly, you must be obedient once God reveals your purpose. You must stay focused and get in shape mentally, physically, and spiritually. Please don't be alarmed at this point. The wisest choice you can make is to love God and obey Him. God knew what gift He wanted you to have. He intentionally placed it inside of you. It is in your mind, spirit, soul, and body, as well as your DNA. In fact, 2 Corinthians 4:7-9 (NKJV) says, "But we have this treasure in earthen vessels, that the excellence of the power may be of God, and not of us." Don't worry about how you will meet the goal. God will see you through and make a way out of no way if necessary. Simply get moving in the direction of what you believe you were born to do.

Glass Slipper Affirmation: I can do all things through Christ who strengthens me. I am blessed and highly favored. God is with me and for me. God's will, will be done. I now submit to God's will for me in all areas of my life and especially in my purpose and my love life.

chapter 3

The Purposeful Princess

> And we know that all things work together for good to those who love God, to those who are called according to His purpose.
>
> —Romans 8:28 (NKJV)

Secret #3: All things work together for your good. Good and bad come together to bless you.

Romans 8:28 says that, "And we know that all things work together for good to those who love God, to those who are called according to His purpose." As we began reading this fairytale, there was no way for us to imagine that the story would end as beautifully as it did. The end of the story is what millions of women live for. From the first time that we read this story, we envision ourselves as the princess who lives happily ever after.

The end of this story is indeed magnificent. The happily ever after ending is so spectacular that over the years, it has changed the lives of millions of women in the world. From the time that women are introduced to this fairytale, the hunt is on. We are looking for the prince. We are looking for him at the bar, in nightclubs, at the grocery store, at the stoplight, at the mall, and in the pews at Sunday's church and other religious events.

Once we find the one we believe to be the prince, we start planning the fairytale wedding. We sit down with pen and paper and we write our first name with his last name, just to see how it looks on paper. We haven't received the ring yet, but we believe that our love will open his heart and change him to be our prince. Sometimes, we know that this strange fellow is not prince material, but we are determined with every ounce of blood in our body to accept him or transform him into a prince no matter what. We believe that our love can change a man into anybody that we want him to be. Many times we waste time, energy, and our youth trying to force a love that is not there.

Let's take a closer look at the main source of Cinderella's pain. Yes, let's talk about that stepmother and those wicked stepsisters. Cinderella's father's choice of a wife who became her stepmother eventually caused our princess a lot of pain. How many times has someone else's choice in life caused you misery? Well, it does happen. Initially Cinderella was probably elated to be a part of a blended family and grateful to have a mother figure in her life, as well as new stepsisters to love and care about. She was probably very happy for her father and their future.

As the story progresses, reality sets in because not only was the stepfamily abusive and mean-spirited, but they were evil. They went out of their way to make Cinderella's life miserable. They abused her, disrespected her unnecessarily, and tried to steal her hope of a bright future. The interesting thing about this dear young woman is that she did not allow them to change who she was. One of the greatest challenges in the world is to go through a storm and not come out bitter, angry, or revengeful, or lose your joy. As difficult as it is, we must learn to let God fight our battles while remaining in His rest. We must be mindful that while we are being challenged we must be careful to not put up a wall around our hearts. The Holy Spirit is available to help protect your emotions and guard your mind, but let there be no wall around your heart. Remember that a wall keeps bad things out, but it also keeps the good things out as well. If Cinderella had given into depression and isolated herself, she may not have met the prince and you would not be reading this book.

There is no indication in this story that she was hurt by any man, but the sisters' mistreatment of Cinderella was very hurtful. Even today, it is a shame how women can be so mean spirited towards each other. It is especially disappointing how some women intentionally hurt other women. It's so sad when biological sisters can intentionally destroy families with petty behavior, jealousy, and a "crab in the barrel" mentality. So many women have shared with me how they have been ostracized by their sisters. At times, biological sisters envy each other's successful marriages, careers, children, and happiness. There are many families where the sisters treat each other worse than strangers.

In this case, we see three females plot to block any chance of Cinderella attending that ball. Well, I'm here to tell you that if God has something for you, then it is for you! No one can stop what God has ordained for you. As we know now, the sisters were able to watch Cinderella's happiness blossom into something wonderful and everlasting. In life you will go through periods of hurt and pain, and sometimes you may be tempted to just shut down. The key is to ask God for the strength to keep going. We have to keep going to give love another chance. Never give up on love; it will be worth waiting for. Sometimes that new chance will not be with the person you want, but it will be better with the person God has for you. So, keep your heart open for true to love to enter in. So many people make the mistake of giving up on love too soon. Usually the one who caused the heartbreak usually goes on with life and never looks back. The one with the broken heart is left to heal their wounds.

The brokenhearted people may decide to not allow anyone into their lives again or entertain the possibility of never letting love in at all. In the meantime, Mr. Right could be staring them in the face, but they are too afraid, timid, and bitter to even have a decent conversation with the man. How many times have we let good ones get away while hanging on to the illusion of an old love with a man who is a complete mess? Start fresh; move on to someone who knows how to treat you and who cares about you and your happiness.

In this story, we see how everything worked together and everyone in some way supported the purpose and fulfillment of Cinderella's destiny. The creatures in the story contributed by escorting her on this special night. The pumpkin from the garden became her coach. Of course, the stepsisters were simply there to motivate her to become a better person and to become all that she was destined to be. There is definitely a reason for the oppressors in our lives. They motivate us and let us know that God is about to take us to the next level. God eventually puts them under our feet and uses them as our stepping stones. Challenges become opportunities, enemies become stepping stones, and setbacks become setups for greatness. God's children always have the victory, one way or another. On that special morning that Cinderella woke up, she had no idea that by the same time the following morning, she would be living in a "dream come true" state of being.

In the story, we see that one of the tactics of the enemy is the constant attempt to keep us busy. How ironic it was that on the day of the ball, the stepmother and stepsisters did everything in their power to keep Cinderella busy. The stepmother asked her to work on windows, drapes, and floors that she had just cleaned the day before.

Oftentimes in our lives, we are caught up in a state of busyness. Let's look at busyness a little closer. Busyness can take you away from the things that are important to your purpose, and keep you from handling your own business. Busyness makes you tired. You become too tired to cook, exercise, think, clean your house, or pick up the phone and check on that friend who was there when you needed someone. By keeping her busy, they were able to prepare for the ball and get ready for a great night. Cinderella had so much to do that she could not even make a dress. The mice loved her so much that they made a dress for her and accessorized it with the bows and ribbons that the stepsisters discarded. Of course, when the stepsisters saw the lovely dress that was made for Cinderella, they destroyed it. They didn't want the accessories, but they didn't want Cinderella to have them either. Their goal was to ensure that she did not attend the ball.

Many times we ask ourselves, "Why do so many good people go through so many sad situations?" I believe that it is in the suffering, or in the taking up of our cross, that we really draw closer to God. For those of us who are controllers, we like to remain in control during challenging times. However, that is the exact time that we should relinquish all control and turn things over to God. God wants us to totally depend on Him. We have to make Him our hero. We cannot take on all of the hardships and struggles of the world; they are too much for us to bear. Just as a good Father should be, He wants us to come to Him and lay our burdens down at His feet. He is in control of it all.

While God is working it out, we must remain at rest in Him. This means that we are calm and confident that God can work it out to our advantage because He certainly will. Jesus can quiet any storm; we simply have to go to Him and ask for help. Life is too complicated and unpredictable to think that we can handle everything on our own. While we are waiting on God, He does a great work in each of us. Sometimes we get stronger. Sometimes we gain the courage that we never had. We grow, we learn more about ourselves, and we build a more intimate relationship with Jesus. It is interesting that we often wait on God to change a situation, but it is God who is waiting on us. He can handle any situation that comes into our lives we just need to totally surrender it all over to Him. God is moved not so much by our tears, worrying, begging, or analyzing the situation. God is moved by our belief, faith, and trust in Him. As 2 Corinthians 12:9 (NKJV) says, "My grace is sufficient for you, for My strength is made perfect in weakness." This scripture will carry you through many storms and even some uncomfortable situations but, in the end you will have total victory.

Surrendering it all assures God that you have total confidence in Him and have peace in the midst of the storm. It is the Holy Spirit who will bring you through a negative situation, and you'll be able to still be peaceful, calm, and carefree. Allow the

Holy Spirit to calm the winds of your raging storm and bring you safely to shore. Remember that Jesus was not the only one who walked on water. Peter was able to walk on water as long as he kept his eyes on Jesus. That's how it is in life sometimes. You know that you must have total trust in the Lord. If you take your eyes off of Jesus, you won't make it. You cannot look down. You simply have to trust Him because Jesus is the only answer to that special prayer. God loves you and cares for you deeply. He created us for His company and pleasure. We are made in His image, and God doesn't make any mistakes. God loves us so much that He gave His only begotten Son so that we could have life and have it more abundantly. Jesus sent the Holy Spirit to enable us to navigate through this life while He sits at the right hand of God the Father. He wants us to praise Him and love Him by spending time in His presence, and permitting the Holy Spirit to give us directions.

The beauty of this story is that when things looked their worst, Cinderella received the help she needed. That is the way divine intervention operates sometimes. He will let us hit the bottom of the barrel or hit the ground, and then He'll raise us up from our ashes. We must trust Him so much that there is no room for any doubt or fear. You can bet your bottom dollar that God will never leave or forsake His children. We simply have to believe beyond a shadow of a doubt that He can and will be on time. He will not let us down or leave us out there without help. It may look like there is no hope, and your mind may be telling you something else, but your heart knows that God is on the case and He's orchestrating things in your favor. While we are waiting, we must remain faithful and know that He is the ultimate fixer. We have to admit that a lot of times, we put ourselves in peculiar situations, and God has to use these situations or tests as teaching moments. It's in our best interest to wait on Him and let Him lead. We will be better off and a lot happier. Our success is based on the faith and confidence that we have in God.

In this story, Cinderella encountered many tests just as we do in life. Here are some of the tests that she encountered.

Would she maintain a good and positive attitude during her oppression? Cinderella had a choice of becoming very rebellious and bitter throughout the story. Her stepsisters and stepmother were holding her as hostage to their every whim and desire. They treated her like a slave and took advantage of her instead of loving her like a family member. She continued to serve them with love in her heart. She did not rebel, and she worked with a good attitude. Interestingly enough, she didn't have a mean bone in her body. She was kind and gracious to them and to her animal friends. What is in the heart will manifest itself one way or another.

When people say that they didn't think another person was capable of any wrongdoing, it is because they do not actually know that person. If you spontaneously curse when things go wrong, then that spirit of vulgarity is in you. If you yell, scream, and throw things when you are angry, that is who you are. Take responsibility for who you are, and work on becoming a better person. Stop blaming others for your behavior. Stop saying that the devil made you do it. If someone drops their credit card on the floor and you do not return it immediately, you have something in your character that is dishonest. In today's society, the dating game can be very superficial. Couples who wish to have lasting relationships need to put the time in to get to know each other for as long as possible before they take that next step. You truly get to know a person only after you have lived with him or dated him for a while. During the dating season, we cleverly hide our faults and portray our best behavior. If a man has a mean streak or an anger management issue, given enough time, it will come to the surface. Now, the question becomes, "What will you do once you see the serpent's head rise up?" It takes a strong person to walk away once they realize that the person they thought was one way is actually another. The truth is hard to swallow sometimes, and some of us grew up hearing these words; "the truth hurts". So I pose this question to you; "Would you prefer to feel good while believing a lie and walking around with false happiness or face the truth and spare yourself future misery?" It is better to wake up to reality because it gives us an opportunity to make a better decision regarding whether to continue with the relationship or not.

When people are dating, everything is lovely and no one wants to show one's true colors for fear of rejection or abandonment. If more people were honest and forthright with each other from the beginning, there may be fewer divorces down the road. At least the couple could see who they are really dealing with, and they could start working on some of their differences, issues, and behaviors. One of the questions that we ponder as we read the story is would Cinderella return evil for evil to the ones who hurt her? She did not do evil things to her stepsisters or their stepmother. She helped them and cared for them as though they did the same for her. How many of us have not been in a relationship, whether it be romantic or family, where someone hurt us or abused our love? It happens all of the time. The key to moving on is letting go and not returning evil for evil.

The Bible is very clear about letting God fight our battles for us. This has to be one of the most difficult requests from God.

Everyone wants to fight their own battles and set everyone else straight. We want to see others suffer or be repaid for hurting us, but that is not the best solution because God tells us in 2 Chronicles 20:15 that the battle is not ours. God says that vengeance is His and that we are to stand still and allow Him to fight our battles for us. This is not easy, but it is the Lord's will even though it's a very difficult position to take, especially when you like to be in control of your life.

We also wonder at one point whether Cinderella gives up her dream of having a beautiful life and finding her true love. She wanted to meet the prince just like everyone else. She was excited about the possibility of going, and she dreamt of wearing a lovely gown to the ball like everyone else. The stepsisters and their mother knew that once the prince saw Cinderella, their chances of being selected as his princess would be over. Sometimes the enemy knows your potential better than you. Cinderella never gave up on her dream. She became sad on the evening of the ball, but I believe that somewhere deep down inside of her heart, she never let go of that dream. Her mind may have been saying, "Everyone is getting dress to go to the ball, and it doesn't look like I am going to meet the prince." God knows how fear and doubt can rob us of our hopes and dreams, but He examines our hearts to see what we are really made of. I believe it was her heart that really got her to the ball. Of course, we all wondered what she would do to her enemies once her dream came true. We see that at the end of the story, Cinderella's dream does come true. She becomes the princess, and heads to the palace to live with her prince.

I have often heard older people say, "Be careful how you treat people. You never know who they may be." I often find it very interesting to see how people treat others just because they don't value them. Have you ever left the house looking a bit simple and plain, and you find that you are treated in a certain way? Have you noticed that when you look affluent, you receive a different type of treatment in department stores or at car dealer shops?

The turning point in the story is when the clock strikes midnight and Cinderella has to leave the ball. If she does not leave immediately, she will be standing there looking quite miserable. In her hurry to leave the ball, she drops one of her glass slippers. She decided to leave it, and it turns out to be a blessing for her. That one slipper is the connection between her and the prince. That glass slipper eventually allows him to know who exactly the young lady was that he danced with all night. She left her mark on that night. She left a clue for the prince to find her and change her future. Divine intervention caused her to drop that slipper; it was all part of the master plan. The prince had to run after her, and she had to leave in a hurry in order to drop the glass slipper. Some things are meant to be and must happen in order for God's will to be done.

One of the most significant events in history is that our Lord and Savior Jesus had to die on the cross. Jesus came to save the entire world, and He knew that He had to be the sacrificial lamb. God gave His only begotten Son so that we could have life and have it abundantly. This is why Christians should have a cheerful and bright outlook on life. Of course, we know that the more we try to serve the Lord, challenges still occur. I'll tell you something. God shields and hides His children because the world system is design to discredit Jesus' and God's works. God protects His children because each of us is a representative or an ambassador of His kingdom. He protects the child and the gifts that are inside of us. God's spirit dwells within His children.

That's why the more time that we spend with Him, the more we feel His presence.

Cinderella was given explicit instructions as to how the night would go, and she was expected to follow those instructions to the letter. Apparently a few things got in the way, such as she was having such a great time, and she didn't realize the time was getting close to midnight. She left the ball at midnight in a hurry, but in her haste she lost one of her glass slippers. That turned out to not be a bad thing but a blessing. A lot of times when something bad happens, we think the worst, but sometimes it works out for the best. Cinderella gave her best to her work and to serving others and so she deserved something good to happen to her.

I believe God honors those who put forth their best efforts in whatever they do. The Bible says that we should work as though we are working unto the Lord. It is good to work with integrity and honesty. Even if no one appreciates our work, we should work like we are working for God. Cinderella worked so hard that she often had ashes on her face, and that is how she got the name Cinderella. From a spiritual standpoint, this is the essence of the story. God took Cinderella's ashes and gave her a life of joy and beauty forever. Yes, God can take whatever dirt, ashes, shame, guilt, or condemnation that you possess, turn it around for your good and have you come out smelling like a sweet aroma. Yes, in spite of how they treat you at work and around town, keep being nice and working hard. Remain humble and do your very best. Work as though you are serving the Lord, and He is your manager and authority. Romans 13 clearly instructs us to respect those who are in authority. Yes, it is true that some are not worthy but, be obedient until God removes that leadership from their position or until he moves you. There is great reward in giving your best. There is great reward in giving your best because God is watching and knows your intentions. When God created us, He provided us with the best stars, sun, and the earth. We should give Him our best work and love and respect each other in a manner that is pleasing to Him. I once heard a pastor say, "God can see through everything except the blood of Jesus." God honors the covenant of His sacrifice of His firstborn Jesus, and we are the adopted sons and daughters of God. There is no condemnation for those who are new creatures in Christ. Praise God, from whom all blessings flow.

Cinderella maintains her same beautiful and loving character throughout the entire story. When her earthly father was no longer in her life, she was able to go on with life and he certainly would have been very proud of her. When there is no father or mother on the scene, God draws us closer to him. All we have to do is seek Him. I remember when I was going through a difficult time in my life, and I was waiting for God to come and save me. Then one day, God revealed to me that He was waiting for me to come to Him and get what I needed. When you have a father who loves you and takes care of you, you go to Him when you need something. Yes, the more that you read your Bible and seek His word and His face, the more God will speak to your heart. God will guide, teach, and instruct you and He will take care of you. How does He do it? God lifts the burdens, destroys the yokes, breaks the chains of strongholds, and fills your life with His joy; then you will have peace. This does not happen overnight. God takes His strategic and on-purpose time to work on hearts, minds, spirits, souls, and atmospheres. This takes time, and He synchronizes the events with great precision.

Cinderella was a true princess in her heart, and the authenticity of it was shining throughout her life. Her father's love gave her the courage to see light at the end of the tunnel. A father's love will do that for a daughter. We need someone to talk to and to encourage us. As it turned out, even the mice had a role in her destiny of forever happiness. In spite of her circumstances she really did believed her dream would come true. Yes, that belief in a, 'dream come true' is what kept the vision alive and got God's attention. God placed in her heart all that was to manifest, and all she had to do was to believe in the dream. God orchestrated that entire night from beginning to end. He created that one special night just for her. When God puts a dream in your heart, it will come to pass. If God has something for you to do, you will do it. I've often heard people say, "If God gave the vision, then He will give the provision."

What were Cinderella's issues, burdens, and yokes? Cinderella was a beautiful person with a pure heart, and she knew who she was. Over a period of time and due to the circumstances, she became a people pleaser. In the beginning, she thought that her love and kindness could change the stepfamily. As time progressed, she began to realize that no matter what she did, it would not change their minds or hearts toward her. She went the extra yard to please them and cater to their every need. She did little things to make them happy. She laughed at their jokes, she brought them gifts, and she sometimes played her intelligence down just to fit in. They still did not like her, and they did not wish her well. They used her, talked about her, excluded her from family time, and were deceitful. Sometimes people play the exclusion game, and we all know that it can hurt. She became frustrated and wondered how long she would have to live like that. I imagine her praying and praying until she would cry herself to sleep some nights. She may have tried to make herself happy by baking. She probably made beautiful, delicious cupcakes to share with her little animal friends, the stepfamily, and the neighbors.

There were times when she remained out of sight and thought it best to be so until she was acknowledged. One of the best and most intriguing things about a woman is that she was made to love, show love, and to receive love. It is true that a woman's emotional health may be based on whether love is flowing in, out, and through her. If there is a wall up for her protection or to keep love out, she may not feel whole, experience harmony or be in balance with nature. Women need to feel loved, appreciated, and cared for. God blessed women when He made us with the ability to love, have deep emotions, and love wholeheartedly. We are auspiciously and phenomenally made. Every woman should be thankful that God made her in such a special and beautiful way.

We all need to be careful not to adapt the people pleasers syndrome. People pleasers need validation, and when they do not receive it they sometimes reject those who are closest to them. When you do not understand what is going on with an individual, you assume that they may be critical, but they may be screaming for attention. When they cannot obtain that attention, they create noise and become a distraction to those around them. Unfortunately, people often abandon the relationship because it becomes toxic and too draining to continue. The life of the people pleaser is sad because they depend on others to define who they are and how they're going to feel.

What the stepfamily did not know was that Cinderella was not actually alone. Although she may have known God on a personal level, there was divine intervention orchestrating her steps behind the scene. They made her life miserable, but that would only be for a short or temporary period of time. All she had to do was hold on to the strength that she was blessed with because her deliverance was on its way. It may have been difficult for her to see, but the trials and tribulations she was experiencing would soon pass away. If she had known God, then she would have realized that the weaker she was, the stronger God would show up in her life.

The day that the prince found Cinderella, it marked a new beginning of freedom and joy in her life. It is a powerful move of God when the yoke is destroyed and the burden is removed in our lives. Before any great breakthrough there is always a test or a season of great challenge. Remember, the bigger the challenge, the bigger the reward. Watch for the signs of the times in seasons of trials and tribulations that you have to endure. The tests that Cinderella had to go through were to prepare her for an awesome future filled with love, joy, peace, and happiness so that she would live happily ever after. Cinderella passed every test that was presented to her. She was clear about her assignment, and she was obedient.

Obedience is a game changer in the movement of God's hand in your life. For years I have been writing this book, and as soon as I would move to write, distractions would come. If you are writing or involved in a project, be sure to stay focused. When you encounter writer's block, and it may come, change your scenery. Take a trip, read a magazine, see a movie, listen to music, or spend time practicing meditation to refresh your mind. Try experiencing something new and wonderful with a friend. If you feel anxious or overwhelmed, perhaps you should try reading or sitting in silence until you feel your peace, focus and calmness return.

Glass Slipper Affirmation: God is perfecting all that concerns me. I let go and let God put His super on my natural. I am beautiful, bold and wonderfully made. Everything is in divine order.

chapter 4

The Transformed Princess

> My Father, if it is possible, may this cup be taken from me. Yet not as I will, but as you will.
>
> —Matthew 26:39 (NIV)

Secret #4: In every life there is a turning point experience when we must seek God for help, and He will be there ready to change and transform our lives.

We know that on one particular night, Jesus went with his disciples to a place called Gethsemane. It was in the garden of Gethsemane that Jesus poured out His heart to God. For Jesus, the garden represented someplace where He could be honest, vulnerable, and authentic with God. The Bible says, "Then Jesus came with them to a place called Gethsemane, and said to the disciples, "Sit here while I go over there and pray." And He took with Him Peter and the two sons of Zebedee, and He began to be sorrowful and deeply distressed. Then He said to them, "My soul is exceedingly sorrowful, even to death. Stay here and watch with Me." He went a little farther and fell on His face, and prayed, saying, "O My Father, if it is possible, let this cup pass from Me; nevertheless, not as I will but as you will.'" Matthew 26:36-39 (NKJV).

In her darkest moment, Cinderella retreated to the garden. In the Bible, there are many great events that occur in gardens. A garden is a place of beauty, sometimes with flowing water, flowers, herbs, vegetables, vines, and fruits. It can be a place of nourishment, restoration, rebirth, and life. How is a garden formed? A seed has to be planted, fed, nourished, and infused with sunlight. We all need light. Jesus is life and light. We plant seeds in our gardens, water them, and watch them grow. We see many blessings in many gardens over a period of time. Gardens are special places that usually offer peace and serenity, solace, and transformation; they represent new seasons of life. Sometimes we refer to the mind as a garden because it is a place where thoughts, ideas, beliefs and dreams originate. We grow and nurture thoughts that can blossom, or they can wither. The story of Adam and Eve in the Garden of Eden describes what happened in their garden and how it altered our relationship with God.

For Cinderella, her garden is where the miracle happened. She entered the garden at the lowest point in her life. She needed a moment to think and let out her frustration. She wept and poured out her heart unaware that her cry was reaching heaven. How do I know this? I know because help came like never before. Oftentimes, help comes when we get out of the way and make room for the supernatural. In the garden, she shared her love, hopes, and dreams with the Almighty who was sustaining her through that difficult season of life. I can only feel that the one in the garden was similar to the personality of the Holy

Spirit. The fairy godmother in Cinderella's life did what the Holy Spirit does in our lives. She blessed and transformed the princess' world. Her life was transformed right before her eyes. I believe that the wand could be compared to the word of God, which can do amazing things especially when we are at our lowest point. In the story, the fairy godmother used everything in her power to create a beautiful experience for Cinderella.

The word of God has healing, restorative, and liberating powers. The more time you spend reading the Bible, the more you will grow in faith. God will reveal Himself to you as you spend time with Him. I really like the part when the fairy godmother used those things surrounding Cinderella to bless her future. Romans 8:28 (NKJV) says, "And we know that all things work together for good to those who love God, to those who are called according to His purpose." The fairy godmother knew that Cinderella was already a princess; it was now time to bring the revelation to the world. The fairy godmother knew Cinderella's heart and needed an opportunity to get her in the presence of the prince. This opportunity is known as a divine appointment. It is also known as a, 'maximized moment'. We have all seen it, where a divine hook-up occurs in someone's life. This appointment changes the parties involved forever. A real prince recognizes a real princess. He is attracted not only to her emotionally and physically but he is especially attracted to her beautiful spirit. He realizes that she is the spiritual rib of his body and that she is the one that he has been seeking. After all, they both have the same spiritual father.

It is important for women to allow God the choice of selecting their husband, if they want His best. God knows which companion is best for you. When you select a companion, you do so blindly; you do not know what is in his heart. God does not look at the exterior; God looks at the heart. God knows whether that man's past is going to dull and hinder your future. There is no perfect man, just as there is no perfect woman. Interestingly, God sometimes joins those with issues together in order to heal and liberate them. I believe that He creates a union of balance, of yin and yang, of give and take, and of harmony. The ideal union is for two whole people to commit to the covenant of marriage. There is a greater success rate of marriages between people who are committed to God, each other and the covenant, than people who are looking for another human to fix them or make them happy. In today's society, marriage is almost synonymous with failure and misery. The numbers don't look good. Surprisingly, there are still couples who are happily married, and committed to one another.

For those who are happily married, they have paid the price and put in the work. Marriages are under attack each and every day. The enemy does not want the family to grow and blossom in the pleasure of the Lord. Couples must keep God in the center of their union because a threefold cord is not easily broken. For those who are seeking Mr. Right, I suggest that you earnestly ask God to select your future husband for you and stay close to the Lord as He creates your ballroom experience. In the interim, stay in God's word and keep your spirit clean and loving, in order to attract loving, kind and caring people towards you. It often amazes me how some of those who are waiting for Mr. Right can be so angry and bitter. I believe that if your spirit, mind, and heart are festering bitter and toxic thoughts, then no matter how together you are in your professional life, you will attract men who are dysfunctional, crazy, dishonest, and abusive. We should practice forgiveness but not allow people to abuse us. If a woman stays in an abusive relationship longer that she should, she becomes wounded and infected. We all know that hurt and wounded people hurt other people. An abused woman gives away her power, she loses her confidence, and her self-esteem is affected. This is why no one should stay in relationships that dishonor them longer than necessary. Learn the life lesson quickly, grow spiritually and move on.

The fairy godmother used the pumpkin, the mice, and other things in the garden to create the opulence of the evening. The glass slippers were carefully chosen because they would be the reuniting factor in this story. In the Bible, Abraham was asked to sacrifice his only son Isaac on an altar. With great pain in his heart and turmoil in his mind, Abraham prepared to sacrifice his son, and then God turned the tide at the pivotal moment by providing another sacrifice, a ram, instead of the boy. The ram and the other glass slipper are paramount in the liberation of Isaac and Cinderella. They were both innocent and part of a greater purpose and plan than what they realized.

A garden represents a space of beauty, growth, refreshment, and transformation. It was the first home of Adam and Eve. God created a place for them of lavish beauty and luscious fruits, vegetables, herbs, and greens in order to live comfortably and healthy. Everything they needed was provided for them. The garden is where the miracle happened. It was in the garden that we see the turning point in the story. Why did it happen in the garden? The garden is also a representation of new beginnings, a place of bountiful vegetation, an overabundance of floral arrangements, and new life. A garden creates an atmosphere of new growth, healing, fresh seasons of life with fresh air. It's God's provision source, and it's a place to be fed and to engage in a level of joy that surpasses the instability of happiness.

Sometimes it's a place to meet the Almighty. The garden was the place where Cinderella could pour out her heart and bear her soul and not be concerned about anyone judging her. It was a sacred place because there were no intruders present to disturb her meditation. Cinderella retreated to the garden when she reached her lowest point, just as Jesus did. They both had experiences there that brought about a transformation in their lives. All things work together for the good of those who love God and are called according to His purpose. Where is the secret garden that you retreat too?

At midnight is when Cinderella underwent the separation of her past from the future that was awaiting her. Depending on your observation, midnight may be considered the hour of power. For Cinderella, midnight epitomized night turning into day or the darkness changing into the light. The Bible tells us that two men of God, Paul and Silas, had been unjustly imprisoned. They prayed and at midnight, and the doors of the prison opened. Yes, the word of God can take you from the pit of a prison to a palace. The Bible tells of how three men, Shadrach, Meshach, and Abednego, were forced into a burning fiery furnace however, the Bible confirms that the Lord was the fourth man who joined them in the fire. When the Lord enters into your dilemma, although you find yourself in the fire, you won't smell like smoke when He brings you out. Suffice it to say, that Cinderella did not look like what she had been through or she would not have caught the eye of the prince.

Another place where a divine connection occurred was during the dance at the ball. It was during the dance that Cinderella and the prince knew that they were meant to be together. I am quite sure that Cinderella allowed the prince to lead as they danced. She gracefully followed as though she was floating on air. Maybe not a word was spoken, just sweet glances and lots of smiles exchanged. In everyone's life, there is that one defining moment that can possibly change everything for the best or for the worst.

Cinderella had favor with the prince, just like Esther had favor with the king. Once the king was in Esther's presence, he was intrigued by her beauty and loveliness. Esther was even able to save her people from destruction because of the favor that she held with the king. Similarly, when Cinderella entered the ball, the prince danced with only her and no one else. Like Esther, Cinderella cared about people and not just about herself. She wanted all of the stepfamily to attend the ball, but they chose to leave her behind and tried to make it impossible for her to attend. It was unfortunate that they perceived her as a threat. Sometimes you can be a threat to others without even knowing it. Cinderella was simply a beautiful young lady who desired to be loved and appreciated.

Cinderella also had something in common with Joseph and the coat of many colors. Joseph was a dreamer, and he was happy and joyful to the point where he was a bit arrogant. Joseph's brothers, like the mean stepsisters, wanted to hold back Joseph from experiencing his dream. The stepsisters wanted to keep Cinderella from her bright future. In the end, both Joseph and Cinderella took the path to a greater and better future. Cinderella learned early on that she could not share her dream with everyone. Of course she wanted to go to the ball. Every single, eligible young woman in the land was invited to the ball. It was the ball of a lifetime, and it was a game changer. The opportunity at stake was great, and she needed to be at that ball. She was excited and was dreaming of what it would be like to dance with a real prince. She could imagine how she would look dancing the night away in his arms. I don't think that she even imagined there was a future in store for her with the prince. Cinderella just wanted to be a part of a beautiful, and memorable evening. She wanted to get out of those dirty clothes and feel pretty even if it was only for one night. She had been excluded for so long, until it became comfortable. I wouldn't be surprised if you can identify with how she felt. She wanted to feel like she belonged. Oh, what a wonderful night she could only dream of having.

Everyone has had at least one special day in their lives that changed the future in one way or another. That one day separates the clouds from the sunshine bursting through. In this case, the night separated the day from oppression to a happily ever after. One great lesson that can be taken away from this entire story is that, "What God has for you is for you." It doesn't matter what the enemy is plotting. If God is going to bless you, He will bless you in front of the enemy. No matter how much the stepsisters and their mother thought they would hide Cinderella from her future, it did not work. Cinderella was unstoppable. She had a cloak of favor on her life, and that was what made the difference.

You may ask, "How can I walk with a canopy of favor over my life?" I would like to provide you with this answer. If you don't see God doing miraculous things in your life, you always feel alone, you have to fight for yourself and if you do not have anyone of power and might in your corner then you need to partner with God in a committed relationship. Your relationship begins by accepting Jesus as your Lord and Savior. You must believe and say that Jesus died on the cross for your sins, Jesus rose from the dead, he is the son of God and that the Holy Spirit dwells in you. If you have taken that step, then you are a new creature in Christ, you have a right to go boldly to the throne of God and ask for His love, favor, provision, and blessing. You are now adopted into His family and that makes you a child of the Most-High God. God is still on the throne, and He sees you and knows everything about you. Talk to God daily and seek His guidance in all things that you desire, and watch God do miraculous things in your life that you never thought could happen for you.

Glass Slipper Affirmation: "The Lord is my Shepherd, I shall not want. He makes me to lie down in the green pastures. He leads me beside the still waters." Psalm 23:1-3 (NKJV)

chapter 5

The Delivered Princess

> Abraham looked up and there in the thicket he saw a ram caught by its horns. He went over and took the ram and sacrificed it as a burnt offering instead of his son.
>
> — Genesis 22:13 (NIV)

Secret #5: We serve an on-time God who is a miracle worker in our lives.

Genesis 22:11–14 tells how Abraham looked up and saw that ram in the bush that saved his son's life. In the Cinderella story, the dance was symbolic of two lives coming together for the first time. This was a magical moment as Cinderella stepped into the prince's embrace. When those two came together, it was a moment that had been predestined long before they ever met. As their eyes locked and they held each other, they knew that their lives would never be the same again and so did everyone else in that ballroom. They had a special chemistry, and it was electrifying. The prince was a little reluctant at first when his father mentioned to him that it was time to select a bride. He wanted to get married, but he wasn't sure he would find the right lady. He had seen many of the town's people and had even grown up with many of them, but there was nothing exceptionally special about the young ladies he saw coming and going each day. He wanted a special lady, a beautiful, compassionate, kind, and caring lady with an enormously big heart of gold for the Lord. He wanted her to be strong yet feminine and sensual. She should know how to speak to people with respect and kindnesses. It was important that she loved children. He knew that he would shower her with gifts and fine things. She should be appreciative of the efforts that others would perform to make her life comfortable. He wanted her to always feel appreciated and loved. It excited him when he thought about how she would reciprocate his love and shower him with the love and affection that he had been longing for. He wanted a lady who was confident and yet independent. Even though she had no prior experience of interacting with the royal staff, he believed that she would embrace the task of learning quickly. He was not concerned about her remaining strong when he was attending to governmental affairs. He would educate her on how to effectively communicate with the staff as well as with government officials and heads of state. He believed that the one he sought was somewhere in that ballroom.

As soon as he had the gala event behind him, he would get out and be with the people. He lived a privileged life, so he welcomed the opportunity to go out and be with the people. Little did he know that his life was about to change forever in a very special way.

Another fascinating thing about this story is that the dance also represents the intimacy between the prince and Cinderella. In the Holy Bible, we see that dance symbolizes rejoicing and celebration, usually after a great victory or time of mourning. I see Cinderella and the prince's dance as a sort of praise dance as their hearts unite for the first time. All of their lives, they dreamed of the day that they would meet the one who would capture their heart. Many women spend their lives searching for that special man and dreaming of that special day, but men search for 'the woman of their dreams'. Perhaps these two young hearts did more than dance; perhaps subconsciously their hearts were knitted together. It was destined that they would only be apart for a very short time. There was a special bond that was formed on that night as the music filled the ballroom and seeped into their hearts. The intoxicating music of the orchestra serenaded the two of them, painting a picture that was lasting, happy, and filled with romance and blessings. They knew before midnight that they wanted to be together forever. They knew that as they stepped in place, their hearts were beating as one. Just as periods of music marks each of the different phases in our lives, the music of that lovely evening was a prelude to a lovely and royal union.

How many times have we all needed a bailout, a lifeline, or God's saving grace? Cinderella's fairy godmother provided her with everything that she needed, but it came with the condition that she would have to leave the ball by midnight. In the rush of the moment, Cinderella heard the clock strike midnight and took off in a mad dash, dropping her glass slipper. Can you imagine how it would feel to be enjoying a beautiful dance with a prince, only to realize that you need to get out of there immediately? She ran out and didn't know what would happen next. She knew that her night was based on borrowed time. She had to go; there was no time for explanations. She had the pleasure of the dance and his embrace. She'd been up close and personal to the man her heart desired. She'd danced with the prince while the stepsisters and everyone else looked on. Some resented them and some admired them as they danced, but then it was over. She looked the part during the dance. Everything about her qualified her to be a future princess.

I believe that she felt comfortable in her short encounter with the prince. At midnight the magical evening came to an end. Cinderella had to once again return to her life of oppression, drudgery, and abuse. She returned, but she wasn't the same. She knew he was the one because during that night, everything that night was miraculous and in divine order. Things fell into place, and she was able to move about effortlessly.

I once heard a spiritual leader say that we know when we have made the right decision and are in a good place when that final decision yields 'total peace'. We have peace about the situation even when we don't have all the details. Cinderella knew in her heart that her life would never be the same, but she didn't know how the story would play out. As the story progresses, the prince is on a mission to find the young lady who was at the ball. He set out with his entourage with a vow to keep searching until he found her. The enemy is always lurking trying to rob everyone he can out of their blessings. This is when the stepsisters and their mother moved into high gear of blocking and overwhelming her with work and distractions.

Have you ever noticed that just as you are about to have a fabulous moment in your life, everything starts to get hectic? The stepsisters were envious of Cinderella because she had captured the attention of the prince. They tried to disrupt her blessings with negativity, disappointment, and humiliation, but nothing could block her blessings. It was already pre-ordained that Cinderella would be the one to marry the prince. No one under the sun could interfere with the victorious ending of her misery or the beautiful beginning of love, marriage, and the awesome future she was about to experience. The prince was on a mission, so when the seeking prince showed up at the right door, everyone rushed to try on the slipper, knowing that it would not fit. Finally, in spite of them trying to hide her and hoping she'd miss this once in a lifetime opportunity, the prince found her. As Cinderella sat down to try on the glass slipper, she was probably nervous and excited at the same time. She was probably expecting something to go wrong, but she was in the right place and at the right time. She would finally have her heart's desire. Her entire life was about to change and everyone in that room knew it once that glass slipper was returned to its rightful owner.

 The enemy knows that you are going to be successful, or else he wouldn't be challenging you. If you have nothing going on in terms of advancing God's Kingdom on Earth, then you do not have to worry about any opposition. Sometimes you may witness others, engaging in evil activities while receiving a lot of great attention. You may wonder how can that be, when that person is not a good person. It is because they are flourishing in a world system that supports cynicism, deceit, negativity and evil intentions. Cinderella was a genuinely sweet, young lady who stood out among the crowd. It made sense that she should win the heart of the prince. Scientifically we know that opposites attract and we are told that spiritually, similar spirits are attracted to each other. The charisma and undeniable chemistry between these two was noticeable to everyone. She knew what the prince should look like because she was raised by a man who had the characteristics of a king. When you encounter a real prince, your life is never the same again.

I know that the main question for many women is, "When will I meet my prince?" All I can say is that it happens in God's time and not in our own. Your job is to work on yourself. When you become so anxious that you run ahead of God, more than likely, you won't get His best. God wants us to wait on Him, but He wants us to 'wait well'. You wait well when you establish godly boundaries to live by when you enter into a relationship. It also consists of investing in the time that it takes to allow God to heal you of all past relational hurts that can be a hindrance to your new relationship. During the wait, take time to get yourself emotionally, physically, and spiritually healthy. You do not want to place unrealistic expectations on the man of your dreams. Many of us in our earlier years diligently sought Mr. Right but, only ran into Mr. Wrong. It seems that when we go out searching for the prince, he escapes us. I've often heard many women say that they met their husbands just when they were not looking for anyone. I believe that God sends the right one to those who believe and trust in Him. As long as the desire is in our hearts to be married, the desire will remain there until it is satisfied, delayed or completely abandoned. God knows what we want and more so what we need. He does not want women pursuing men. God wants His Kingly sons to pursue their future wives.

God's timing is impeccable. So many times we pray for God to move in our lives now. We beg, we pray with tears streaming down our faces, we bargain with God, we promise God, we cry uncontrollably, and then we fall asleep. Our God is a sovereign God; He can do whatever He wants to do when He chooses to do it. We must be patient and while realizing that patience is a virtue. You just need to believe that good things and people are worth waiting for. We cannot rush God or force an issue to be resolved any quicker than He would have it be solved. As a matter of fact, I have found that God moves best when I take my hands off of the situation. I pray on it, and even though I want things to move faster or in my direction, God does it best and knows the right timing. When I was growing up, the senior citizens used to say, "He may not come when I call Him, but God is an on-time God." This means that God does not work on our timetable, but on His own schedule.

While Cinderella was praying about her situation, this is what she was probably doing.

1. She sought the Kingdom of God, so that all things could be added unto her.
2. She maintained a good attitude despite how the stepsisters and their mother treated her.
3. She served others.
4. She nurtured her friendships with the critters of the house.
5. She kept her vision alive in her heart and mind.
6. She stayed in shape so that when her opportunity came, she would be healthy and look gorgeous.
7. She had a plan as to which dress she would wear to the ball, but she ended up wearing a prettier dress.
8. She did not speak negatively about her oppressors; she spoke positively about her life.
9. She focused on things that were good, uplifting and promising.

10. She actually put enthusiasm and excitement into helping the stepsisters get ready for the ball.
11. She did not let them see her sweat or operate from a position of defeat.
12. She kept her composure until she entered the garden.
13. She continued to work hard and do her best.
14. She was honest with herself about the situation.
15. She was willing to step outside of her comfort zone.
16. She always believed that something wonderful was about to happen in her future.
17. She did not operate from a position of guilt, shame or condemnation.
18. She was very clear about who she was.
19. She stayed focused on her job even when she didn't look or feel her best.
20. She knew that once she was delivered, she would not look like what she had been through.
21. She learned some life lessons throughout the entire ordeal.
22. She was a true friend to the friends and accountability partners that she did have.
23. She was courageous throughout the situation.
24. She worked on renewing her mind so that she could change her world.
25. Even on days when she didn't know how she was going to make it, she believed that she would have the victory.
26. She entertained herself by singing, dancing and imaging a beautiful life.
27. She dreamt of her heart's desire.

God's Timing

God is an on-time God. Sometimes it looks like He is not answering our prayers, but He most certainly is. "So why is He silent?" you ask. God is often silent when He is working our situation out behind the scene. He is positioning people to assist you with your situation. He is speaking to hearts. He is encouraging those who may have to represent you in court, or approve your bank loan, or change your medication to a more effective one. God knows what He is doing. He is the greatest source of love that there is. God really does love us, and He really does want to bless us with more than anything that we could ask for or imagine, just as it says in Ephesians 3:20 (NIV). "Now to him who is able to do immeasurably more than all we ask or imagine, according to his power that is at work within us."

Here are some ways that God answers us with His responses to our prayers.

1. Yes – the time is right and we are blessed with our heart's desire.
2. No – we may want something, but He knows it's not good for us.
3. Not now – it's not a denial, it's just not the right time.
4. Silence – He's not ignoring us, He's quietly working behind the scenes on our behalf.

We must have faith when we pray and then patiently wait for God to answer. He is adjusting and putting an array of plans in place for our benefit. Here are some things we can do while we are waiting on God to answer our prayers. We are to let go and let God. God will not have you ask Him to handle a situation and then have you take control of the same situation. He does not need your help to solve any of your life problems. He created us and knows what we need. We should pray that God's will is done in our lives. If what you are begging and crying about is not within His will and purpose for the advancement of His kingdom, then He will not grant it to you. God placed many talents, gifts, and treasures within you, and they are to be used to praise Him, glorify the Lord, fulfill the purpose of your life, and advance the kingdom of God.

Here are some practical examples of prayers that may not be answered. You want a certain romance to begin and blossom into marriage. It is not happening because he is already married with a wife in another state. You want a job position because the salary will end all of your financial issues. It is not going to happen because you want that position for the wrong reasons. Additionally, you need more time to learn how to stop overspending and manage what money you do have. You want that home in that affluent neighborhood. It may happen, but not until God is ready to bless you with it. He knows exactly when you will be ready to not only appreciate that type of home, but you'll also take care of it. God will bless you with a nice car, but as long as you are coveting something that someone else has, you have the wrong motive and He will not fulfill that desire. You get my point. Trust God because He knows what is best for you. Proverbs 3:5–6 (NKJV) says, "Trust in the Lord with all your heart and lean not on your own understanding; in all your ways acknowledge Him and He shall direct your paths."

Why Some Women Will Never Meet the Prince

1. Some women have had some bad relationship experiences, and they will never trust anyone ever again. There are walls around their hearts. Yes, I know that the wall is there to protect you from getting hurt again, but you are not really living. If you cannot love unguarded and freely with common sense, you cannot receive all that God has for you. Presently, in this society not many people can love with total abandonment; it's too risky and costly. The wrong relationship can cost you everything—your youth, time, money, sanity or even your life. Remember that if a wall is blocking and protecting the heart, nothing can get in—not even love. A wall is a wall. The wall goes up because you are afraid to be hurt again. Fear is not of God, because the Lord did not give us a spirit of fear but of power, and of love and of a sound mind according to 2 Timothy 1:7.
2. Some women and men continue to play the victim game, and this role allows them to keep on attracting partners who force them into a victim's position. We must see ourselves as victorious and not as victims.
3. If you are not happy with yourself and with life, no one can make you happy. You must first become that which you seek. You must be willing to give what you are seeking.
4. If you want a great relationship, then you must treat yourself as you want to be treated. You cannot disrespect yourself and expect someone to respect you. It's true that we teach people how to treat us. We must continue to love ourselves and realize our worth. Know your

value. We are God's children, and we deserve the best that God has to offer. Teach people how to treat you well. Set up some boundaries in your life; it will force people to respect you and treat you right.

5. This next point took me a while to learn, but it was a lesson well learned. Your love cannot change a person. People do what they want to do. If the man does not return your telephone call, it is because he does not wish to speak with you. When love is new, some men will call you multiple times a day. Once the prize has been won, things may change. Those same men may no longer be interested. Actually, for some people the game of love is all about the chase and the capture. Isn't it interesting how a man can be obsessed with a woman and then lose interest once they have had sexual relations? That's because the woman was a challenge in the beginning. Once he gained access to her virtue, he no longer finds her intriguing; she is no longer a mystery. She is no longer inaccessible, but rather is one who has been captured. Women are emotional and nurturing human beings. There are often feelings of rejection and great pain after realizing that he is no longer interested. If you think about it, perhaps he never intended to stay. Some men will hold on to you and monopolize your time for years, hoping to find someone better. Sometimes they will play one woman against another. I could never understand why some women attack and confront, 'the other woman' when the problem was clearly created by the man. Women have to learn to love themselves and maintain their freedom while holding on to their integrity.

Providence has a way of working the unexpected out in our lives. Sometimes God works in mysterious ways. When the clock struck midnight, Cinderella made a mad dash down the stairs in an attempt to get to her coach and make it home. Fortunately, as she was running down the stairs, she lost her glass slipper. As she progressed, everything turned back to the way that it was originally. The horse, the pumpkin, and the mice all became as they were before the magic of the evening began—except the other glass slipper.

God intentionally will give us something to keep as a reminder of the promise. Sometimes it's a dream, a song, a book, a promise in the Bible, or a child. Yes, a child left behind from a relationship can sometimes be the key to the promise. Look at how many famous people have changed the lives of their parents. Very often it's the life of that single parent, who had no other choice but to raise that child and give parenthood 100 percent without knowing where and what the future held. Do you think that President Obama's mother had a clue as to who her son would one day become? At the end of a long and very emotional night, all Cinderella had was a glass slipper. At least the glass slipper let her know that the night was real and it was evidence of an evening she would never forget. She didn't realize the impact that glass slipper would have on her future but, she was hopeful that it was the prince who retrieved her lost slipper and not someone else. The night had actually happened, and she was one of the main characters in a fairy tale setting. She left her mark, and it was a special night. Now she had a token of that night, and she would treasure it no matter what happened next. All she could do was hope for a brighter future and sit back to watch the events play out. The mere fact that she was blessed to meet the prince meant, there must be something else good on the horizon. Somewhere in the back of her mind, she knew that she would see that other glass slipper again. What she didn't know was that the glass slipper would change her life forever.

What tokens do you have that let you know that God isn't finished with your situation? Sometimes a glass slipper can be a beautiful child who was part of a relationship that has ended. At first you may not see the blessing, but then you may notice that God deposited a gift in your child that can change your life forever. The dream of this book has been with me for over twenty years, and the vision of it has tied me to a dream come true. If you are holding on to a dream, or if you are holding a key to a dream, keep holding on and working toward that dream. If we believe it and trust God, then we will surely reach our greatest moments.

The Glass Slippers

There had to be two glass slippers because all shoes come in a pair, and at some point there had to be a match. There would have to be a validation of Cinderella being the right young lady. It is ironic how the moment of great victory was proven in front of the very ones who tried to tear her down. God says in Psalm 23 that He will prepare a table for us in the presence of our enemies. Yes, God will let you have the victory in front of your enemies. Haters don't like to see innocent people become successful. Let God fight your battles for you. No one can correct an act of injustice better than God. In the story, the fairy godmother blessed Cinderella with slippers that were customized just for her. They were made in her size, for her comfort, in a very special material that only her fairy godmother had access to. These were no ordinary slippers. They were made of glass! Have you ever walked in shoes made from glass? Furthermore, have you *danced* in glass slippers? I would think that they are especially delicate and have to be handled with care. Most things that are made of glass are shipped or moved about with a note or label that states that they are, 'fragile'. Yet Cinderella danced, ran down the steps, and headed back to her carriage on cobblestones, gravel floors, wood floors, and hard dirt, and those slippers remained intact.

Let's look at what happens once the glass slippers are separated. One slipper is with the prince, and he knows that the slipper belongs to the love of his life. He knows that she is a very special lady because no one else wore glass slippers to the ball. She was wearing a custom-made slipper, and no one else had a pair that even came close to the beauty of her slippers. He also knows that it is not normal for someone to take off in such a hurried fashion after making a great love connection. He was completely consumed with finding her and he wasn't going to stop until he did. Now that the woman of his dreams existed, he only had eyes for her.

The other slipper was with Cinderella. If she would have left the ball prior to midnight, then losing her slipper would not have been an issue. Once it was midnight nothing else remained except the glass slipper. The coach, the dress, and the horsemen are all gone. When Cinderella removed the one remaining slipper she may have been reminiscing about the unique experience she had with the prince. To see the prince and have a dance was enough to get her excited. But now, she wondered what was going to happen next, since the slipper had been left behind. How different would things have turned out if she'd left before the stroke of midnight? Instead of letting the "what ifs" drain away all the wonderful excitement of the evening, she chose to dance around her room as though she was still locked in the arms for the prince. Remember, if a man really wants a woman, he will do whatever he must do to find and claim her. Cinderella had enough memories to keep her calm while she anticipated the possibility of seeing the prince again. She did not have to try and make anything happen. She did what we should do and that is to believe that good things will continue to come into our lives and that challenges will come but they will also pass away.

The Miracle

In this story, the glass slipper that was left behind is synonymous to the ram in the bush. What is your glass slipper? The favor of God is the secret weapon! It is the unexpected twist in the story. It came from out of nowhere. In Genesis 22:11-14, Abraham looked up and saw the ram in the bush that saved his son's life. In the case of Cinderella, that glass slipper changed her life forever. The glass slipper represents the essence of Cinderella; it is the one thing that people remember about her. Wherever she goes, she is remembered by how she makes people feel. When a man is courting you, the manner in which you conduct yourself should make him want to be with you as much as he can. Start off the relationship with teaching him how to treat you and not compromise your standards. You should be good to him, but don't give him privileges that he does not deserve without committing to you. It is not fair for you to be the only one cultivating the relationship while he does little to secure a committed relationship.

What does it mean for those who retrieve the lost slipper left behind? It is assurance that you were there and it was not a dream. You just changed his life, and it was wonderful, a dream come true. He will never be the same again. Whenever he thinks, hears, smells, or sees you, all he feels is love, and he unmistakably knows one thing, he must have you. It's sort of like a heart that experiences the highest level of love and intimacy; it can never go back to mediocre love. We cannot fool the heart to accept that which is less than the best that we have had. Once you have experienced the best, you cannot settle for less. You cannot ever fool your mind to satisfy your heart. After all, the heart knows.

The glass slipper is a reminder that the prince's desire to find the perfect princess has now been satisfied, but she got away, and now the prince must go find her and claim her love once and for all. Many will try on the glass slipper, but the prince will not be fooled because he knows who the real princess is. He has to find her, see her face, look into her eyes, and have her try on the slipper. Because of the great prize at stake, the Master will only make one of a kind pair of slippers so that only one unique person can fit each pair. Cinderella was given the slipper as her insurance card. If you remember, everything turned back to the way that it was at midnight, but the glass slippers remained the same. The slippers are the determining factor and the key to Cinderella's and the prince's happiness. The fairy godmother performed magic to create all of the elements that contributed to the bliss of her night. Everything was temporary, but the slippers were permanent. The glass slippers represent love, hopes, and her dreams for Cinderella. They represent the desires of her heart and the greatest blessing for her future.

You too have a secret desire in your heart that you wish would come true. That wish has a sacred place inside of you. It is so special and sacred that you may never share or articulate to anyone what your wish or desire actually is. In a lot of cases, there is a lot work and that may also be tied to that wish or desire. For that reason, some people will never have their fondest desire, no matter how hard they try or wish for it. Remember, faith without works is dead. I believe that Cinderella's wish came true because she was pure of heart and forgave her offenders. She was very optimistic about her future. In order for her to get through every day, she had to maintain a positive attitude. Everybody needs somebody to encourage them and Cinderella had help too.

Sometimes a situation can be so impossible that we have no choice but to finally, 'let go and let God' because we are about to give up on everything or make some very poor choices. When we are in difficult situations, we want God to fix things immediately and make us feel happy again, but sometimes He will leave us in a situation until we begin to grow, change, and desire His will. Cinderella decided to use her energy to focus on something bigger and brighter than the continuing environment of living with her stepmother and stepsisters. It's absolutely amazing when God puts His super on your natural. God has all the power to do for you what you can't do for yourself. God has the ability to bless you beyond what you can imagine. God not only wants your life to be blessed, He wants you to love Him, and to enjoy the love of the right man who will know how to love you. This is why you must depend on God.

As you know, the prince sets out to find the owner of the lovely slipper. There were a lot of women who tried on the slipper and every one of them wished their foot would fit, but it didn't. They push, they squeeze, and they tried to maneuver their feet into it. They could not get their feet into it because the blessing was not for them. Do not be afraid that you will lose your turn or your blessing. Keep working hard, believing in and talking to God. Speak God's word back to him because His word will not return to Him void and without a promise kept. The Lord let us know in Isaiah 55:11 (NKJV), "So shall My word be that goes out from my mouth. It shall not return to Me void, but it shall accomplish what I please, and it shall prosper in the thing for which I sent it." God has a blessing that He has prepared just for you. Have faith, keep dreaming, believe and keep praying. He hears you, and He is coming. He is an on-time God, and He wants the best for his children.

When the prince arrived at the house of the stepsisters, they tried to keep Cinderella in the back. They tried to undermine her presence. At this point, they are now overwhelmed with fear. They fear that Cinderella is the young lady who took up all of the prince's time at the ball. They were afraid she would become his princess and leave them. What would happen if she punishes them for every mean and hurtful thing that they had done to her? The stepmother had sufficient reasons to be afraid because she was going to be stuck with her two annoying, useless daughters. She was hoping that one her daughters would capture the prince's eye and that the chosen one would be her ticket to the palace. She is so disgusted with how this is all turning out. She was accustomed to using people; it was not unusual for her to look for opportunities to use anyone and anything to her advantage. She wondered if Cinderella is chosen, she will bring them along. Why, even if they are servants, it is still better than how they are living now. At this point in the story, something exciting is about to happen. Cinderella will finally be happy and loved beyond measure. How many women ever really meet their God selected princes? I believe that many will once they surrender to God's plan of love for their lives.

Glass Slipper Affirmation: "I am trusting in the Lord with all of my heart and not leaning on my own understanding. I am acknowledging Him, and He is making my paths straight." Proverbs 3:5-6 (NIV)

chapter 6

The Chosen Princess

He who finds a wife finds a good thing, and obtains favor from the Lord.

—Proverbs 18:22 (NKJV)

Secret #6: The husband will seek, find & pursue his wife.

The Bible states that he who finds a wife finds a good thing. I would have to agree that God wants every man to have a virtuous woman as a companion. Ladies, you are not to hunt for a man. God wants your husband to find you. As previously mentioned women wish for the day of their dreams, but men dream of the woman of their dreams. Men like to be in control. They are hunters by nature. It is natural for your future husband to search for and pursue you. The woman who relies totally on God to provide her prince, has the upper hand in love. Partner with God so that He may bless you with a godly husband. God knows your man better than you do. God knows about his baggage, He knows about his intentions, and He knows his heart. God will send the right man to you at the right time.

In the interim, we need to work on becoming whole women. We need to heal from those past toxic relationships and learn to love ourselves. Life has shown us that God has given us a blueprint of recognizing the ideal mate, but life can present us with many twists and turns, and sometimes we even stray away from God. Many times due to the pressures of life, a woman may choose the wrong mate because she became impatient and did not trust God's timing. We are pressured by the chronological and biological clocks of our bodies and by society. Many times, we choose the wrong mate because we did not follow the plan that God presents in the Bible. What is the plan? The plan is to seek God so that He may position your future husband to seek and find you. We must also consider why our approach to marriage is not always the best way. How does God feel when we put a man above him in terms of love, dedication, pursuing and seeking his affection with relentless abandonment? If you haven't realized it by now, we serve a jealous God, and He must come first. When we put a man before God and worship the idea of making a man our god, while building our world around him, it is nothing more than idolatry. God does not want us to place anyone or anything as a priority over Him. Yes, we should love our husbands and strive to be the best wives that we can be, but to marry a person simply to live a fairy tale life is entering into a relationship that is headed for trouble.

We often see women who absolutely lose their minds while planning the wedding. The financial burden that weddings create is almost scandalous. The amount of effort and coordination that it takes to host a wedding is paramount as well as is a major production. Frequently, we ask ourselves, "Is she more concerned about the wedding or the marriage?" I assure you that there is a big difference. The bride who is conscious of the vows that she is about to profess and declare before God and man is on the right track. Who cares if the cake costs one thousand dollars if the groom will not be faithful to you? Does it matter if the bridesmaids' dresses are silk or taffeta, if one of the bridesmaids slept with the groom? Can you see where I'm going? The focus needs to be on the marriage and not solely on the wedding. Weddings are becoming huge debt traps. If more couples focused on securing a down payment on a home instead of having a great big party to impress people, then things might make more sense. I suggest that the consciousness of weddings versus prenuptial counseling requires much thought and soul searching. If there is one point that I would like to stress concerning the union of a man and a woman is for them to truly understand that they are entering into a covenant. The covenant requires both people to be committed to the marriage. Today, marriage is viewed more like a shopping experience. You try it out and if you don't like it, you go back and make an exchange. With that in mind, there is no need to wonder why the divorce rate is so high and continues to rise.

Now, let's explore the characteristics of a true prince. The reason why some men are not able to recognize a princess or know how to treat a lady like a princess is because they do not possess the qualities of a true prince. Matthew 7:15 (NKJV) states, "Beware of false prophets, who come to you in sheep's clothing, but inwardly they are ravenous wolves." The prince in our story is a real prince. What is a real prince? First of all Ladies, not every man that you fall in love with is a prince. There are three types of men in the world. There is the "No Way Prince" (NWP), the apprentice prince, and the prince!

The NWP will never be a prince. He is a user, he has nothing going on, and he is probably looking for you to take care of him. He may take you on a few nice dates and then you'll notice a change in the way things are going. He lives from day to day and has no intention of making a commitment to you. He may even live at home with his parents. He cannot keep a job, and he perceives everyone as being the problem instead of examining himself. Staying in a relationship with this type of man will more than likely pan out to be a wasted investment of your time if your objective is to be married. He is not the one to create a future with you. If you are the kind of woman who enjoys caring for and nurturing people, then you will find yourself naturally attracted to this loser because you feel that you can encourage him to be somebody. The NWP will wear you out. You probably love to care and nurture people, and so you naturally attract this loser. Do you remember what Jenny told Forrest Gump to do when in direct contact with combat? She said, "Run, Forrest, run!" Well I am telling you to run, girl, run! The NWP is a frog, and if you kiss him, he will not turn into a prince—you may turn into a frog too.

Let's take a closer look at the NWP because sometimes he looks and acts like a prince. You have to be careful. The NWP is dangerous and sly. This is the man who does all of the right things in the beginning. He calls you twice a day and can't live without you, so he says. He is attentive and appears to want the same things that you do in life, but he is a user and doesn't plan to stay around very long. He may even be married. Did he give you all of his telephone numbers or just a cell number? Have you been to his house? Is he still living with his sister or mother? The NWP is also a master liar, and as we know, one lie begets another. The NWP may also be on a time schedule. Does he only see you on certain days of the week, and never likes to change the schedule? He also likes to stay in and claims to be a homebody. You'll find him making excuses as to why he doesn't want to go out. After all, dating is expensive and you may not be the only one he is seeing. He often suggests that you stay in and cook which leads to another night of you serving his needs. Please protect yourself from this user. You will never receive an offer of marriage from this man. He probably is already married or separated, and he's just using you to fill the void. Dating this type of man will certainly test your intuition. As time progresses, you will sense that something is not right, but you may not be able to immediately put your finger on it.

As time progresses, it will become clear that he is no prince but is rather a mistake. He is afraid of commitment and will do whatever it takes to not meet you at the altar. He is a dreamer with no plans to ever settle down. He doesn't save any money or make plans for his future. If you have a child with him, you may end up raising the child alone. Why do you think we have so many single mothers? A large number of women do not even receive child support to help raise their children. He is useless, and if your car stalls, he cannot help you out with money or service. His main issue is that he will not take responsibility for his life. He is always chilling out or checking out the scene. He can make a great friend or hangout buddy, but he will not make you a good husband. There are just too many women out there who are giving the NWP privileges that only a husband is entitled to. If you are one of these women, eventually you will become impatient and start pressuring him to step up to the plate. Unfortunately, you have already set up the relationship where he does not have to make a commitment to you. It's the same as when you dress in such a revealing way that the man doesn't even have to use his imagination of what you look like undressed because you're showing the goodies. If a man truly loves you and his intentions are honorable, then he'll be willing to wait to receive those husband privileges by putting a ring on your finger. The NWP will hold on to you for as long as he can, which is dangerous because if you want children and a future, he is not the one. If you want children and you're still at the child bearing age, remember that you have a biological clock that is ticking, even right now. Do you hear that ticking sound? That's your life, and he's wasting your time. He has no problem wasting your time and money, eating your food, and wasting your youth. This man can frustrate you to no end. Save yourself the frustration of being in a dead-end relationship. Oh, and did I mention how he will suck the life out of you? You will age before your very eyes. Remember, most of the time he just wants 'the cookie'. The good news is, you own 'the cookie' and you are the one who is in control. Do not give your power away. So, now that you know how this man operates, please continue to ask God to bless you with the spirit of discernment and wisdom as you socialize and date. Remember to guard your heart and do not allow anyone to waste your precious time. Scripture instructs us, "Above all else, guard your heart, for everything you do flows from it." Proverbs 4:23 (NIV)

Now, let's explore the characteristics of the apprentice prince. The apprentice prince has great promise, and one day he will become a prince. His relationship with God and his life experiences will turn him into a prince. He will become a prince before your eyes. I guess it's sort of like when the princess kissed the frog in another story. The good news is that he has potential, and he is headed towards becoming a prince. Now, here is the deal. You need to set a time limit on this relationship because he may need extra time to find himself. At times he is a sad character because he may be all over the place. He may try his hand at different jobs and careers. He's human, and so he may try to pull a fast one on you every now and then. This man could date you for several years before making a solid commitment. He's not so much afraid of commitment as he is afraid of disappointing you. He is afraid of failing within the relationship. He may have been hurt or even deceived before. He is independent and does it his way in his time. This man is really a good man with a lot of potential, but he needs God. He may need a personal encounter with Jesus, and by that I mean he will need to come to the end of himself in order to allow God to help him get it together.

You may be wondering right now, "How can I get my hands on this man?" Sit down and I'll tell you. You may already know him and not realize it. He's usually somewhere in your perimeter of associates. He may be in plain sight. Sometimes he lives in the neighborhood, he attends your church, or you see him at the grocery store. He may not be your brand of eye candy that you are normally attracted to but, he's a handsome man when he pulls it together. Once he decides that you are the lady of his dreams, you are in for a wonderful experience with a guy who will want to protect, profess, and provide for you. This is a great thing but one of these qualities is always a little tricky. Yes, you guessed it, providing for you could be an issue for a while. Love and romance takes money to make things go smoothly. The apprentice prince is a work in progress, and this is good sometimes because you may need time to work on yourself as well. No one is perfect, but with love and respect synergistically working, you two will succeed. Once he finds you, and you're the right one for him, together you can make it work. The apprentice prince puts in the work. An apprentice usually has a mentor. There's a man who made a difference in his life. There are some godly men around him. He may have single friends, but he wants a family of his own where he is the head and the provider. He has his eye on the prize, and as soon as he gets it together, he's coming with your other glass slipper.

Ahhh, and then there's the prince! The prince loves God, and when he marries you, he will love you as Christ loves the Church. The prince may also be described as an, 'Ephesians 5 Man'. He is loving and caring. He wants to settle down, and he doesn't want to play any games with you. He will find you. You do not need to go out to find him. You should go out to have a good time, and when the time is right, God will send him to you. Sometimes he is not the most distinguished man in the world, but the heart of the prince is priceless. He is a keeper. He will raise his children with discipline and respect. He is no pushover, and he is the head and the leader in his home. He prepares for your future and is not afraid to give you all of himself. He is a real man and likes to do manly things, so sometimes he will need a little breathing space. He is committed, so you will not have to worry every time he leaves the house. He is not going to cheat on you. Not every man will cheat on his wife. Yes, there are still many men who honor their marriage vows. This is the man who can give you a lifetime of love and happiness, and he is in it for the long haul. The true measure of his love will be proven when things get rough. Trust me, every marriage has ups and downs. True love can survive any storm. It may not be easy, but love still conquerors all.

Let's study the prince in our story. It was his father who initiated the search for a wife. He knew how he raised his son, and he knew when it was time for his son to take a wife and build a future for himself. He knew that the princess would find her way to that ball. The million-dollar question is, "How did the prince know which young lady would change his future forever since all the eligible women were invited?" He knew because God put the knowing in him. When God guides the righteous man to choose his wife, God points him in the right direction. God designed it so that the man would create his family based on His guidance. He is supposed to be the head of the household and love his wife as Christ loves the Church. On the night of the gala, there were many beautiful young ladies in attendance, but once he held Cinderella in his arms, he knew that she was the one. What were the telltale signs? He recognized her by her virtue, essence, and aura. We all have a spirit and countenance about us. It's sort of like a light or vibe. It's similar to when you walk into a room and the atmosphere changes. The atmosphere can change in several ways to excitement, sadness, friction, or happiness, but it will change because we all have energy. Hopefully when you enter a room, you bring light and positive energy. The prince had the gift of a discerning spirit. He could detect her loving spirit and sensitivity and those qualities drew him to her like a magnet. Let's closely examine the prince and his actions. First of all, he had the support and encouragement of his father to take a wife. Today, the average man does not try to encourage his sons to get married, but rather to play the field for as long as possible. The prince's father was wise and knew that it was time for his son to seek a wife. It was not only his age that determined he was ready. His father had taught him about responsibility and maturity. He had observed him long enough and came to the conclusion that he was now ready. The prince knew exactly what he was looking for and the character and qualities he wanted his princess to possess. There were hundreds of young ladies who responded to the invitation of the ball, but the prince danced the entire night away with Cinderella.

You have looked high and low, seeking out the prince. At times you have compromised your happiness, pride, joy, and you've lost your money seeking men who looked like princes and told you that they were princes, but at the same time, your intuition told you that they were not princes.

Here are the top characteristics of a prince.

1. He loves God, and he strives to love you as Christ loves the Church.
2. He will not do anything to intentionally break your heart.
3. He takes his vows seriously, and he is faithful to you.
4. He is a man of integrity; he says what he means and means what he says.
5. He is a provider who respects his and your money. His financial security is important to him.
6. He practices a continuous effort to live healthy and be physically, mentally, and spiritually wholesome.
7. He respects you and shows it.
8. He supports and encourages your dreams.
9. He makes time for you because you are important to him.
10. He pours into you as you are pouring into him.

Earlier we examined the love between Ruth and Boaz. We clearly saw how Boaz possessed the qualities of a true, 'Ephesians 5 Man'. An, 'Ephesians 5 Man', will love you as Christ loves the church. He will respect and love you in a righteous and holy manner. He will protect your purity and he will marry you once God has shown him that you are his help mate. It is a beautiful experience when an, 'Ephesians 5 Man' marries a, 'Proverbs 31 Woman'. This relationship combination is created to advance God's Kingdom while fulfilling God's purpose in their lives. This power couple will bear fruit and will be blessed to be a blessing to others. Their love is steady, strong and sure with God in the center of it all. This union is created to give God the glory. Perhaps, you may know such a couple.

Glass Slipper Affirmation: I am a new creature in Christ and the best is yet to come. God knows the desires of my heart, and in due season, he will deliver to me the perfect God-loving, Ephesians 5 husband who will love me as Christ loves the Church.

chapter 7

The Blessed Princess

To give them beauty for ashes.

—Isaiah 61:3 (NKJV)

Secret #7: God will give you beauty for your ashes, turning your misery into joy.

Cinderella went from kingdom living in her father's house to the pit with a stepfamily that made her home life oppressive. Eventually, she went to the palace with the man of her dreams. She possessed the true essence of a princess. This became evident when she faced her saddest moment in the story. Cinderella believed she was different from her stepsisters, but by the time those stepsisters turned her world upside down, her self-confidence was weakened. In spite of it all, she remained a lady. Even when she was in the depths of despair, she retained her composure as a true princess. I can only imagine how difficult life was for her, but inspite of it all she remained humble, kind, and considerate and she did not repay evil with evil. She prayed for her enemies, but did not allow resentment to take up residency in her heart. Although she was free in her spirit, she needed to be removed from that situation. The best way to keep her spirits up was by entertaining herself and by being friendly with the critters of the house. As a result, they too were loyal to her. I learned a long time ago to be kind to people because you never know who a person really is until you need them. It is best not to burn your bridges because you never know when you'll have to cross them again.

You can just imagine how Cinderella may have felt while trying to cope with three women who obviously meant her no good. She probably woke up early each morning wondering if something out of the ordinary would happen for her. Each day was just like the previous day; she had to encourage herself and do the best that she could.

When we are mistreated, betrayed, or deceived, God will step in and fight our battles for us. We do not have to seek revenge. We should keep our eyes on Jesus and then let go and let God handle our affairs. The reason why we should not intervene is because we never have all of the pieces to the puzzle. For instance, sometimes God allows difficulties to come to strengthen us and take us to the next level of life. Sometimes we need to grow in knowledge, courage, strength and wisdom. It is God's will for us to look to Him to supply our every need. When we finally reap success and the pain is gone, we should give God the glory and praise His holy name. Regardless if we are unfaithful to God, He is faithful to us and He is always in control. He knows our hearts, and He loves us unconditionally and provides for us just as He promised in Philippians 4:19. Sometimes it might look like God has forgotten about us, but if we hold on and keep believing, He will surely make everything better. When that day comes, the enemy will look on and realize that the plot to hurt a believer has been cancelled. God will bless the believer to continue to rise to great heights, in spite of it all. Only God can make your enemies your footstool, every opposition an opportunity, and every challenge a stepping stone for greatness. Don't worry about your enemies and all of their evil plans. God can and will turn it around. He can even set it up where your enemies can serve you and protect you against other adversaries.

In today's time, Cinderella would have been considered blessed, anointed, and set apart from the rest. She had to go through the misery of that situation to get to the place of happily ever after. You really need to hold on and keep believing, and surely something wonderful will happen for you. We cannot rush God; He is an on-time God and knows what is best for us. Keep loving Him, thanking Him, and talking to Him. He created us to be His friends, and children and in fellowship with Him. God is our Creator and wants us to be obedient to His Word. There are supernatural experiences He wants us to have. If God gave us everything we wanted without being prepared, then those desired things could reap havoc in our lives. It is so easy for us to think God is withholding good things from us. Never forget that God already sees the beginning from the end. He is a loving Father who does not want you to go astray. Can you imagine how great it would be if every day, we showered Him with the same amount of love that He has for us? We could never out give God because He so loved the world that He sacrificed His only Son for us to have life, and have it more abundantly with a promise of His salvation. The fact that He woke you up this morning is proof that He loves you and has a plan for you today. You just have to seek Him as we are told to do in Matthew 6:33.

When Jesus went to be with His Father in heaven, He sent the Holy Spirit to look after you and care for you. The Holy Spirit is your comforter, guide, teacher, helping hand, mentor, and spiritual advisor. He's the one who is with you always to protect and care for you. He is the One doing the work in the earth. When your prayers are being answered it is the Holy Spirit who manifested the answer. As the story is told, the fairy godmother used her magic wand to transform her critter friends into blessings for Cinderella's good. Her magic wand may be seen as synonymous with the word of God which changes the atmosphere and can change people and situations. It was easy to transform Cinderella's world because she had a date not only with a prince but with her purpose and destiny.

You may wonder what happens if you never meet your prince. I'll tell you the biggest secret in this story. The reason that you cannot find him is because he is supposed to find you. You simply have to get ready and trust God.

This story is about an amazing transformation that creates an auspicious blessing just as Isaiah 61:3 (NKJV) says, "To give them beauty for ashes." This story tells us that Cinderella worked really hard and often had cinder dust ashes in her hair, on her face and on her clothes. It was because of those ashes that the stepfamily actually gave, 'Ella' the name of, 'Cinderella'. Isn't it interesting how people can give you a name that they have created for you? A name can be a very special and symbolic characteristic of who you are. As in many Bible stories, God changed the name of the blessed one to a name that was synonymous with their purpose. God changed Saul's name to Paul, Jacob to Israel, Sari to Sarah and Abram to Abraham.

Throughout the Bible, we see that God changed many people's names to mark a new beginning in their lives and to add purpose and significance to their futures. Ask God to bless you with a new name, or research the meaning of your current name. I am quite sure that your name has a special meaning and that it may even be tied to your purpose.

Now, let's take a look at those ashes. Our ashes may be the pain, burdens or sorrow that we bear. They could represent a wicked past, with lots of dirty little secrets, negativity, and bad memories, but God can certainly clean us up. He would prefer for us to come to Him just as we are, dirty, sinful and with anything else that is in our lives that is ungodly. He said that when we go through the waters, we would not drown, and when we go through the fire, we would not burn. In other words, He is saying that we will not look like what we have been through. Trust me when I tell you, only God can do that for you. How many times have you seen people who have struggled with alcohol for years and it is evident that they are broken? What about the person who has been battling substance abuse and they look beaten down? Sometimes they are a young person, but they appear much older than they actually are simply from the years of abuse. I am quite sure that when Cinderella's coach arrived at the palace, she did not look like she had just cleaned a five-bedroom house, ironed everyone's clothes, assisted with hair and makeup, and cooked that evening's meal. Once her transformation occurred, she had no more ashes. She looked beautiful, her face was glowing, and she looked radiant. That's what God does for those who believe in Him and love Him with all their hearts. It's amazing how many benefits you get to enjoy when you give your life to God.

What the fairy godmother was to Cinderella is similar to what the Holy Spirit is to us today. Cinderella needed supernatural provisions and that is what the fairy godmother provided for her. Cinderella also needed the instructions that the fairy godmother gave her that led to her destiny. The Holy Spirit supernaturally infuses us with the power to accomplish God's will. He was sent as the true comforter sent to us by Jesus. The Holy Spirit guides us, protects us, provides for us and He is the ultimate comforter. If we follow His instructions we too will reach our destiny. It is also a blessing to have a spiritual godmother or godfather in our life. There has been one woman who has made an amazing impact on my life. The person that made a tremendous impact on my life is my sweet, dearly departed grandmother, Inez. My beloved grandmother was the most generous person I have ever met. She gave everyone the best of herself. I couldn't understand why our home in Brooklyn, New York, was always filled with people all weekend long. She prepared delicious Caribbean food on Saturday mornings, but long after the food was gone, the doorbell was still ringing. It was only after I matured that I realized people stopped by for more than food. They came to our home for kindness, advice, friendship, and companionship, and to feel loved. My grandmother instilled in me that I mattered. She thought me that with God I could rise to great heights. She taught me to be a compassionate, gentle, calm yet powerful leader. She deposited many nuggets of wisdom within me that I still value today. She taught me how to pray, talk to God, and trust Him. Most importantly, she loved me unconditionally. The Holy Spirit is the one that will orchestrate that divine appointment between you and your mate. He is the one who will lead you out of the darkness and into the light of life. John

14:26 (NKJV) says, "But the Helper, the Holy Spirit, whom the Father will send in My name, He will teach you all things, and bring to your remembrance all things that I said to you."

At times the prince in our story reminds us of Jesus. Jesus is portrayed in the Bible as a humble, wise, obedient servant of God, the son of God, a teacher and a lover of mankind. Even today, His greatest characteristic is that He loves us unconditionally. When we go astray, with the help of the Holy Spirit He draws us back to Himself. To sustain a loving relationship with Jesus, all we have to do is stay connected and remain in fellowship with Him. In this story our prince certainly proved that once he had an encounter with Cinderella, he was not going to let her go. He went after our girl just as Jesus goes after any missing sheep. Our prince was obedient to his father and sought his princess at the recommended time that his father suggested. Once Cinderella and the prince married, they lived happily ever after. You would have to imagine that being married to such a man was absolutely amazing. Proverbs 18:22 states that a man that finds a wife finds a good thing and he obtains favor from the Lord. If a woman is not prepared to be a wife, then she is not the best mate for marriage. Being a wife requires dedication, wisdom and a loving heart with a great will to forgive when necessary. She also has to be strong, respectful and certainly not be a victim but walk in the confidence of the Lord. Every day we encounter beautiful women who could possibly make wonderful wives but, they are hindered by their own baggage and the unwillingness to forgive themselves and others. Being a wife is not easy, but if she is with the best man that God chose for her, their union can be beautiful in spite of the ups and downs of life. Wives are busy people. Wives cook, clean, work outside of the home, have careers, raise children, do community work and still need to satisfy their husbands' needs. Husbands need love, sex, respect, delicious homemade meals, encouragement, emotional support and wives need to handle that. Every woman who desires to be a wife to a kingdom husband should pray for deliverance from any unforgiveness that she may be holding onto. Unforgiveness is definitely a blessing blocker. Holding onto any negative emotions is a sure way to block God's blessings. How can you possibly forgive someone who has hurt you beyond repair? I can assure you that there is only one way. You must ask the Holy Spirit, the comforter, to heal your spirit and help you to forgive the one who has offended you. Some hurts you cannot forgive on your own. Only God, Jesus, and the Holy Spirit can help you forgive when it is hopeless. The enemy would love to see you take matters into your own hands and seek revenge, but then you would be out of God's will. You see, it is all a trick to keep you in bondage. You have to release the pain, hurt, disappointment, guilt, shame, and condemnation in order to allow God to prepare you for your new prince.

When you ask God to help you forgive, it takes a little while for your emotions and mind to catch up with your act of obedience. You cannot understand it, but one day you will wake up and move forward in a new, liberating way. I find it necessary to inform you that forgiveness is not predicated on your feelings. If they were, we would never forgive the people who hurt us. It is an act of your will that you give the Holy Spirit permission to help you forgive. Once you do that, you're acting out of obedience to God. He is the One who requires us to forgive others just as we want Him to forgive us for the wrong things that we do. You can get on with your life, and you don't have to look back. The best part about forgiveness is that you can still love some people, but love them from a distance. You don't have to give them your attention or interact with them. Release them and set yourself free. You are the one who is now able to fly away. Yes, you may remember what happened, but the intensity of that past pain is truly diminished and you will know that your healing is in progress. Once again you will be able to give and receive love. You may welcome love again. This is a sure indication that you have forgiven the offender and you can move forward and be happy again. You will feel like whatever happened is behind you. Resigned yourself to enjoy your life and not look back. You have wasted enough time trying to figure it out. You may never understand why and how someone you cared for was able to hurt you. Interestingly, the offender is not the one who needs closure and doesn't even care about those who were hurt in their path. Remember that people who are hurting are very capable of hurting other people, and sometimes they don't even realize what happened and how much damage they have caused.

I am happy to say that given enough time, the Lord will help you to forget the details of what happened. It is also very helpful when we stop playing the offenses over and over in our minds. Let's not give any more power or attention to that which has already stolen time and some of our youth from us. The secret here is that if we trust God, then in due season He will make it up to us. God will replace what the locust has eaten up or in other words, God will replace that which has been stolen from us.

Happily ever after represents a lengthy period of happiness and joy. The prince was a child of a king. He was a genuine prince. Men ruled by a king are influenced by the king's behavior. Men who honor God make better husbands. Isaiah

9:6 and Ephesians 5:25 state that a husband should love his wife as Christ loves the Church.

God knows your situation. He is watching as you navigate through life. When you go to God, speak to Him about everything that is in your heart, not just what you see in a book written by someone else. Written prayers can be wonderful, but God wants to hear from you. There is no need to say a prayer that was written for a lot of people to recite. When we go to God, we should be honest and transparent because He is the omniscient God anyway. God wants to have a relationship with us. That involves dialogue and conversation. We have to learn to engage in true communication with God. Communication involves speaking and listening, and it is best when it is balanced. You talk, and then you wait for a response. God may not respond immediately, like two humans talking back and forth to each other. However, you should be listening and expecting Him to answer. When the time is right and in His time, He'll answer. Sometimes we are so busy and distracted that we cannot hear from God. Reduce your level of noise as well as ignore those many distractions so that your communication with God may flourish while allowing you to follow His lead.

In order for Cinderella to experience beauty for her ashes, she had to encounter her fairy godmother. Before that amazing encounter, I'm quite sure that Cinderella had moments of self-defeat along the way. There were days when she might have wrestled with feelings of resentment over the way the stepsisters treated her. Did they think just because she was nice and forgiving, she was a fool? Why would people mistreat someone who is kind and caring? How could her stepmother sit back and allow her daughters to treat a family member so poorly? To be honest with you, those adversaries were there to take her to the next blessed level of her life. This may have been one of her prayers.

Dear heavenly Father, I humbly come before you. I want you to know that even though my new family has hurt me, I forgive them because you have forgiven me of my sins. I work hard and I try my best to please these ladies, but they continue to treat me unkindly. Why do they reject me so? Dear Lord, please speak to their hearts and encourage them to be kind and understanding with me, if that is possible. I feel so misunderstood, and I am trying to remain kind and loving. Dear God, I would love to go to the prince's ball. I would love to meet the prince and have him look at me and tell me how beautiful I am. Is it possible that I can meet the prince, or maybe have a dance with him? I offer my hopes and dreams to You, Lord. The Bible says that you know the desires of our hearts. Well, the desire of my heart has always been the same. I want to love and be loved. I desire to have a blessed marriage with a godly man. I want to be the one that the prince chooses as his princess. I believe that I am qualified to be a princess because my heart is filled with love for you and even for those who come against me. Thank You for listening, God. I love you and I praise your holy name. Amen.

Like Cinderella, we all have ashes. As you know by now, Cinderella's name actually means, 'Ella' with ashes, and we know that in the end, she was given beauty for those same ashes. She was so compassionate that when she left, she took some of the little critters that had been kind to her to the palace. This is why we should be kind and respectful to others, because we do not know what significant role they will play in our lives. We all know at least one person who had humble beginnings, and then his or her future brighten up. Once these people started moving up, they took some people with them. We must be selective when choosing the right people to enter our space and world. Not everyone who is around you is happy for your success. Let us continue to seek the Lord's face and pray big, bold prayers. Our God is a big God who wants to see us happy and successful. You may have heard it said that some people are in our lives for a reason, a season, or a lifetime. I personally believe when people show us who they are, we need to believe them. It is to our disadvantage for it to take three or four times of them showing us. The first time really should be enough. All you need to keep in mind is that, they may get by doing what's wrong for a season, but they won't get away with it forever. God has His own way of dealing with these people. Leave them in God's hands and you just keep being the person God wants you to be. God will not allow the enemy to use His children indefinitely. In the interim, we should continue reading and studying His word. The word of God provides restoration, hope, faith, and love.

Let's take a closer look at some of Cinderella's relationships in the story. What about those wicked stepsisters and their mother? Here we have two mean-spirited, trifling sisters whose bad behavior was unfortunately encouraged by their own mother. You may say, "Oh, it's just a story." However, these sisters live among us. We see on television, how women display their cut throat tendencies over men who do not qualify to be of prince quality. They attack and undermine each other as well as family members. If a woman will be deceitful to her own flesh and blood, what would she do to others? Women know how to hurt other women by spreading lies, stealing their lovers, or by spitefully rejecting them. There is also evidence of bullying and isolating each other. Yes, women know how to hurt other women because we know how emotional and needy we can be. Some women love attention more than others and another mean spirited thing that women do to each other is play the exclusion game. No one likes to be left out or isolated. Such an act says that you are not with us, you are not good enough, and they don't want you to be in their circle. Some women can put up with this behavior for years, but it ultimately tears down their self-esteem and creates resentment and bitterness. In a lot of instances, this type of behavior opens wounds that never closed, based on earlier relationships with parents and siblings. Women hurt other women socially, in the work place, in politics, in the church, in school, and in love. Overall, women need to learn how to respect each other better.

God has blessed women with a special God–given power. We must educate ourselves about the power we have as we consider companions or connect with possible soul mates, they should resemble Jesus. Jesus is the one true Prince. This hunt to find a prince has turned our society into a culture of idolatry and deception. The pressure and the goal of finding the prince has often forced so many women into a corner of wrong decisions and a loss of time, energy, youth and sometimes their lives. God wants every woman to have a husband if that is her desire, but because of our world system, some women will never get married. The good news here is that Jesus wants you; He is the epitome of royalty and He can fulfill your every need. The blessing is that when we seek God with our whole hearts, this gives Him an opportunity to bless us with a chosen earthly husband by choosing the right man and setting up the divine appointment for that man to meet us. We serve a God who loves to communicate. We should talk to God about our desire for a mate. The most important thing is for us to be open and submit to God's will. Whenever we can come to the position of allowing God's will to be done, He will connect you with the person who is right for you. Our focus should not be on hunting for a man, but to prepare ourselves to be ready when he is delivered to us. By focusing on Jesus it provides us an opportunity to declutter, de-stress, and decompress from the cares of the dating world. This freedom enables us to relinquish the obsession of hunting for a man.

Your spirit, soul, mind, heart and emotions may not be creating a vision of God's best husband for you. I cannot over emphasize enough for you to ask God to have His way and let His will be done. In the interim, ask God how you can prepare for the husband that He is sending to you. Get ready for the God-chosen husband. Get yourself together—mind, body, spirit, heart, and soul. Detoxify and renew your mind, cleanse your body with healthy food and purposeful self-care practices. Upgrade your relationships by forgiving those who have offended you and by surrounding yourself with positive people. If you have an ungodly soul-tie relationship that is hindering God's blessings, it must end. Such relationships are not in God's will and do not advance your purpose. They actually block and delay, 'The One' from being drawn to you. We must break negative spirituality, emotionally draining and toxic soul-ties that do not honor God. We must sever and separate ourselves from soul-ties that are not in the will of God for our lives. In order to break such connections we must acknowledge their presence in our lives, confess and repent of our sins, forgive yourself and the other person, separate or disconnect from that connection. Most important, we must renew our minds. Remain in prayer, speak a soul-tie breaking prayer over our life and get ready for some amazing blessings. Remember, we want to remove anything that would stand in the way of our future husband finding us or being attracted to us.

God wants us to focus on the marriage instead of the wedding event. Our focus needs to be prioritized by God's order of marriage. Most of all, we must give our love to a true prince and not a frog that will never be a prince. We must attract the prince and not chase the frog that is disguised as a prince. A wedding that has no future is a waste of time and money. Such an event can create a lifelong impression of failure and a memory of disappointment. So now that you know the truth, you can properly prepare yourself for the prince who will eventually become a husband who will love you as Christ loves the Church. Remember to respect God's timing because it is impeccable.

The palace is the final and greatest destination for Cinderella. The palace represents a majestic place of luxury, magnificence, and dreams coming true. It declares to the world that she will become princess of the palace. The arrival at the palace symbolizes that she has arrived and stands by the prince's side. One day they will rule together. He will be the king, and she will be his queen. The palace is a place where royal families live, grow, love, and take care of those for whom they are responsible. People respect the palace and those who live there. It is even an honor to work in the palace. The responsibility and leadership of the king and queen of the palace is paramount to the success of the kingdom and all who serve and reside there.

It was interesting but not a surprise that Cinderella took her good friends, the mice, cat, horse, birds and dog with her when she headed to the palace. She probably was very relieved to leave the wicked stepsisters and their mother behind. As you can see, she is an amazingly loving woman, and that is the very reason she was blessed. Before she could receive her royal crown, she had to bear her cross. So many beautiful people encounter delays, disappointments, tragedies, and setbacks each day, but they have to carry on. What we can learn from Cinderella was that her heart was that of a princess long before she became one. She never stooped to the stepfamily's level. She dealt with criticism and abandonment, but she never allowed it to make her bitter or spiteful. I believe that when we are going through our trials and tribulations, it is nothing more than a test to see how we will respond to adversity and how we will move forward in life. It is a test to see whether we cling to Jesus or become hateful, and whether we become angry with God.

Life can be very difficult especially these days, and sometimes we ask God why do we have to endure such trials and tribulations. I believe that God allows certain situations to occur in order to make us stronger, help us grow, and take us closer to fulfilling His purpose for our lives. I have noticed that some of the most successful people in the world have had very sad and trying times during the earlier stages of their lives. It is during great times of suffering that many seek God and gain a more intimate relationship with the Lord. It is during times of abandonment, rejection and insecurity that uncovers the essence of who we are that draws us closer to God. We know where to go to be comforted and loved. No one else loves us like God. We know where there are open arms waiting to embrace us and provide the assurance that we are loved and not alone. How many times in the scriptures does God tell us that He will never leave us or forsake us? Not only does He tell us that He will always be there, but He tells us to have courage, to trust in Him, and to know that He is working everything out for our good. In Psalm 18:2, God assures us that He is our strength, protector and deliverer. Romans 8:38, tells us He will be with us forever. Nothing can separate us from the love of God. Hebrews 8:12, says God will forgive our sins and remember them no more. He tells us that when we accept Jesus as our Lord and Savior, ask for forgiveness, and repent for our sins, God then forgives us. God will then forget what we have done and cast the memory of our sins into the sea as far as the east is from the west. The mere fact that He is willing to do that for us is enough to shout about. We do not have to be burden down by the guilt and shame of things we have done. He wipes your slate clean and gives you a second chance. Isn't it just wonderful to know that God does not highlight your past? There are times when you come across someone who takes the liberty of reminding you of your past, what you did or how you used to be. People may not give you grace, but God does.

God makes it clear that He forgives us; unfortunately we are the ones who will not let it go. How arrogant of us to continue to hold on to that which Jesus died to free us from. Jesus died on the cross, and the least that we can do is say thanks to Him at each available opportunity. We must forgive ourselves, although that can sometimes be more difficult than forgiving other people. There are times when our minds condemn us and we feel miserable about the sins we have committed. I know for a fact the Holy Spirit can accomplish what you cannot. He is just waiting for you to ask Him. You will be amazed by what the Holy Spirit wants to do in and through you. We must move on while serving the Lord and doing what we came to earth to do, which is His work. God made us to be in fellowship with Him and to love and honor Him, just as we wish to have companionship and friendship with others. God wants to have a relationship with us. He wants us to talk to Him and seek His guidance as we go about our busy days, making decisions and choices. Our lives should be one long prayer with God, day in and day out.

One night soon after they arrived at the palace, I can imagine Cinderella having a little talk with God.

Dear Father God,

Oh, how I love you. For so long I have wished for someone to love completely and for someone who loves me unconditionally and exactly as I am. Thank You for blessing me with my heart's desire. I bless your holy name, dear God. Father, I thank you and I say to God be the glory for this marvelous thing that you have done in Jesus' name. Amen.

For us modern women here are some tips to consider as you prepare to be found by your prince. Wait well and prepare to be the wife that he is looking for. At this point, I would like to highlight the scripture which says, "A man that finds a wife finds a good thing and he obtains favor from the Lord." I want our future brides to understand the portion of this scripture that is often overlooked. This scripture clearly states that your husband will obtain favor from God because 'you' are in his life. Do you understand how powerful that statement is? God is letting you know that you are so important in the marriage union that He brings favor to the man because of you. 1 Peter 3:7 (NIV) says, "Husbands, in the same way be considerate as you live with your wives, and treat them with respect as the weaker partner and as heirs with you of the gracious gift of life, so that nothing will hinder your payers." God is clearly saying that He does not honor the prayers of a husband who does not honor his wife. Finally, God commands that your husband love you as Christ loves the church. With such a love, you will feel comforted and secure submitting to your husband as God commands us to do.

Glass Slipper Affirmation: God knows the desires of my heart. He already knows whom He has chosen as my future husband. There is no need to be concerned about whom God has chosen as my true companion. God is in control and the best is yet to come. I trust God and I am waiting well with joy and great expectancy.

Ladies, the first step to living your best life is to accept Jesus Christ as your Lord and Savior. If you have never done so and you are ready to turn your life over to God, please say this prayer of salvation and watch God work miracles in your life.

The Prayer of Salvation

> Dear Father God in the kingdom of heaven, I need you and your love. I believe that Jesus is Your Son and that He died on the cross for my sins. I believe that Jesus died, was buried, and rose again from the dead. I believe that one day Jesus will come again. Dear Jesus, please come into my heart. I make you my Lord and Savior. I am yours forever and happily ever after.

Once you have said this prayer out loud, you are a new creature in Jesus Christ! Now that you have made this commitment, things will get interesting. The enemy does not like it when we officially join the kingdom of God, and he will try to convince you that you are still a mess. How will he do this? The enemy will attack your mind. At this point, you will need to do a few things to protect your peace.

1. Read your Bible daily; even a few minutes a day is a blessing.
2. Join a Bible-teaching and Gospel-preaching church.
3. Talk to God every single day, and don't forget to thank Him for your many blessings. Thank God for what He has done, is doing and is preparing to do in your blessed future!

Remember daily that you are a child of God and that Jesus died on the cross so that you could have everlasting life, and have it more abundantly!

Good night Princess, sleep well you have a bright and exciting future ahead of you.

Testimonials

Testimonial of Queen Maria the wife of King Lance

Our Favorite Scripture: "The kingdom of heaven is like treasure hidden in a field. When a man found it, he hid it again, and then in his joy went and sold all he had and bought that field. Again, the kingdom of heaven is like a merchant looking for fine pearls. When he found one of great value, he went away and sold everything he had and bought it." Matthew 13: 44-46 (NIV).

Do you believe that God chose your mate for you?

It is without a doubt that GOD chose my mate for me. I used the prayer model from my church to declare myself worthy, ready, and already full with the Love of GOD. Then I asked GOD for signs that it was HIM and not my will to choose my mate that HE would send. Then I listened for GOD to confirm it.

When did you know in your heart that God meant for you two to be together?

Love is friendship on fire. The moment we met we both knew that we were already in love. We spent almost 9 months becoming the best of friends first virtually, before actually meeting. It was also love at first sight. The physical attraction came only after the spiritual, emotional, mental, intellectual, and communication attraction was tried and tested to be true. The strong friendship we built initially was the foundation for the love to stand firm on.

What one thing confirmed for you that your husband was, 'The One'?

I asked GOD for three signs in 3D that he was "The ONE". I received three supernatural signs to confirm this: 1. His name Lance was the same as my Father Lancelot. 2. A Scripture we were reading on 9/24/2010, also stated that the prophet Haggai asked a question on the same day. "On the twenty-fourth day of the ninth month, in the second year of Darius, the word of the Lord came to the prophet Haggai, This is what the Lord Almighty says: Ask the priests what the law says: If a person carries consecrated meat in the fold of his garment, and the fold touches some bread or stew, some wine, oil or other food, does it become consecrated? The priests answered, No." Haggai 2:10-12 (NIV). While we were reading this together, we were shocked when we realized it was the same day that was noted in this scripture. 3. Both of our Parents were married on the same day, same month and in the same year which was 10/8/1955.

Testimonial of Queen Patrice the wife of King James

Our Favorite Scripture: "Be anxious for nothing, but in everything by prayer and supplication, with thanksgiving let your requests be made known to God." - Philippians 4:6 (NKJV)

Do you believe that God chose your mate for you?

Absolutely! After a difficult divorce, 15 years of being single and raising my children, and only after ensuring they were on solid academic, emotional and spiritual footing, did I begin to date. I knew that I wanted a life partner and I wanted to be married. After a while, I began to feel as if God had forgotten me so, I decided I would go online and help God help me find my husband. I dated three men, one of whom was a pastor. While I had some fun moments, something was always off. One lonely night, with tears in my eyes and in my pajamas I asked God asking why no one wanted me. What had I done? I had always carried myself as a woman of God. I did not want to be alone. I told God in that moment I was done. It had to be Him that helped me, not the on-line dating services. As I cried I said, "God I give it to you". I literally raised both my hands and began to thank God for my life. In 2016 while attending a dinner in Washington D.C. my best friend Kathy introduced me to James. Kathy explained that he was a widower. It was a casual greeting and we all continued to mingle. James and I exchanged numbers. A month later we gathered at Kathy's for Sunday brunch. After a lovely social we headed in different directions. It was approximately 5 minutes after leaving he called and we talked his entire drive to D.C. We stayed on the telephone for 5 hours! We have spoken every day since.

When did you know in your heart that God meant for you two to be together?

Memorial Day weekend 2016 James invited me to come and visit him in Maryland. He purchased my train ticket and booked my hotel. It was while we were visiting the Lincoln Memorial he told me that he loved me and he wanted to be with me for the rest of his life! At that time he asked could we be in an exclusive relationship. No one has ever asked me that before. He also told me that he was celibate and that he had only been sexually intimate with his wife and the next woman he was sexually intimate with would be his wife.

On Monday May 29, 2017, my James got down on one knee and proposed to me at a family Memorial Day celebration! He had told everyone in the room via email except me. That was one of the happiest days of my life!

On September 9, 2017, we became husband and wife and I know with 100% ontological certitude that our meeting and marrying was God! When I surrendered and had disconnected from the men I sought out for myself, is when God said, "Now you're ready!" My husband is my God given gift!

What one thing confirmed for you that your mate was, 'The One'?

There were MANY things that let me know that he was the man God has chosen just for me but one thing that stands out for me is when he met my children he told them he loved me and he wanted to make sure that the three of us (Malcolm, Breyana & I) knew how much he loved us. The word 'us' did it for me because I prayed for someone who loved me but who adored my children and I had that!

My husband and I during our morning devotional have found several scriptures that speak directly to us. The scripture that resonates with him is II Timothy 4:7, "I have fought the good fight, I have finished the race, I have remained faithful."

Testimonial of Queen Evelyn the wife of King Dave

Our Favorite Scripture: "Unless the LORD builds the house, the builders labor in vain. Unless the LORD watches over the city, the guards stand watch in vain." **Psalm 127:1 (NIV)**

Do you believe that God chose your mate for you?

Yes, I believe that our love connection was predestined by God! The year was 1985 and I had just started my new job in New York City and commuted from Queens on the NYC subway every day. Although I seemed happy, had lots of friends and a full social calendar, I was lonely. I felt finding a suitable partner seemed elusive and impossible. Lots of prospect but in end most men fell short. I was starting to feel I would never find love. On one of my morning commutes, I noticed a very handsome man across from me. We met officially a few days later and immediately had a lasting connection. The rest as they say is history.

When did you know in your heart that God meant for you two to be together?

During our first year of dating, one day in a subway train going to work Dave looked at me at said, "I think that I love you" and I said "I think that I love you too". From that day forward, we just remained committed to each other and our relationship.

What one thing confirmed for you that your husband was, 'The One'?

That was 33 years ago! We are married 31 years with two beautiful accomplished daughters. Although we can say we lived happily ever, all the glory goes to God. Dave is my soul mate, but I am confident without God as the head of our household, we would never have made it. We are eternally grateful that in a big lonely place as New York City, God brought us together and has kept us together.

Testimonial of Queen Barbara the wife of King Dan

Our Favorite Scripture: "Trust in the Lord with all your heart and lean not on your own understanding: in all your ways acknowledge him and he will make your paths straight." **Proverbs 3:5-6 (NIV)**

Do you believe that God chose your mate for you?

As a young girl, I had prayed to God that I might one day have a God-fearing, nurturing and loving husband. Like most young girls, I dreamed of being married and having a family. When the Lord sent Dan, the Holy Spirit revealed to me that this would one day be my Boaz. We were so compatible...like God had ordered our steps. I just loved being around Dan, listening to him and spending time with him. He was so thoughtful. He carefully made plans for our lives and how we would spend our time together.

When' did you know in your heart that God meant for you two to be together?

Our friendship and love have lasted since we met in 1972 and became college sweethearts in 1974. Later, we were married in 1985, and God blessed us with our son, Griffin, in 1989.

What one thing confirmed for you that your husband was, 'The One'?

I really can't say that it was any one thing that made me realize that this was in fact my Boaz. It was a collection of great things. Dan treated me so very special. He was just so loving, kind and considerate of my feelings.

When we were young college students, I observed Dan from afar and genuinely admired him. He had so many good qualities. He was an independent thinker and didn't follow the crowd. He had good judgment and Godly wisdom. He had a passion and love for music -- particularly Jazz. He was an avid reader and spoke French fluently. One high school summer, he lived with a family in the South of France and spoke only French. Dan had a phenomenal voice and was in the Northwestern University Community Ensemble Baptist Choir. He was just a very well rounded, God-fearing young man, who never indulged in drugs. Later, I realized that he was heavily influenced by his loving dad, who was a pillar in their community.
It was so many things, which attracted me to my Boaz. It made me realize that surely Dan is the person, which God wanted me to spend the rest of my life with. I praise the Lord for ordering my steps and giving me such a wonderful friend, lover and husband!

***

Ladies, it has been an honor and privilege to share this letter of love with you. I hope that you have been blessed by this message and that there is a happily ever after in your future. May you allow God to move on your behalf as He auspiciously orchestrates the approach of 'The One' that He has chosen just for you. May you rejoice as God transforms your life by exchanging your ashes for His beauty. May you completely surrender to God's will as you turn those past hurts and heavy burdens over to Jesus. Continue to diligently seek the Lord and you will surely find Him. Don't wait for Him to come to you, you go to Him. Stay beautiful and prepare yourself for your kingdom husband. I cannot promise that everyone who reads my book will get a husband because God does not promise us marriage in the Bible. I've check. I just know that God's covenant of holy matrimony blesses whom He joins together as husband and wife. The purpose of this letter has been to inspire you to believe and receive the spiritual wisdom, discernment, and patience needed to attract the man of God that the Lord has chosen for you. Understandably, you may have to wait a little while for your Boaz to find you. No one can tell you when or where he will appear. When he does find you and has proven himself worthy of your love, please treat him like the king that he is. Honor your husband as he honors God. Cherish his heart and his love as it is not to be taken for granted. A godly man's love is a treasure. You have tried love your way and now I am suggesting that you try it God's way. Give God's advantageous and fulfilling approach to love a chance because God honors those who are obedient. When we are obedient the rewards are indeed abundant. There is guiltless pleasure and joy in pursuing love and marriage God's way. So, let's wait well, have patience and have great expectations as we keep our eyes on the Lord. Trust God with all your heart and soul. Straighten your tiara, get out there and live your best life while God is working it out. Enjoy the freedom of singlehood while you have it. Travel, socialize, serve others and love yourself. Try new things and experience life in a new and exciting way. Love does not have a color, so experience new cultures and welcome people from different countries into your world. You have a vision of your future husband but, he may not come in the package that you have imagined. Remember, David in the Bible did not look like a king when he was tending to the sheep but he was still destined to be a king. I believe that when God blesses us it is above and beyond what we have imagined or asked for. The amazing blessings of God can be breathtaking, blissful and humbling. A kingdom husband has a heart for God that is equipped and capable of changing your life to the happily ever after season that you desire. Please continue to pray for the men of the world so, that God will continue to shape them into kingdom husbands as His daughters are waiting for them to come. As you are waiting on your kingdom husband remember that you are blessed with the love of God who is protecting, guiding, guarding and taking care of you. You are blessed because Jesus sacrificed his life for you on the cross just to secure your salvation. You are blessed because you have the Holy Spirit as your comforter. I love you and I too will be waiting with you. We'll wait well together. With love, Janice

> "The Lord bless you and keep you; the Lord make his face shine on you and be gracious to you: the Lord turn his face toward you and give you peace." Numbers 6:24 -26 (NIV).

About the Author

Janice G. Johnson grew up in a loving Bajan home in Brooklyn, New York. Her favorite island in the Caribbean is her mother's home of Barbados. She has been a member of the healthcare industry for over 35 years in the area of Information Technology. Janice holds a Masters of Public Administration: Health Services degree from Fairleigh Dickinson University in New Jersey. She currently freelances and volunteers as a public relations & marketing consultant for non-profit, private and corporate business organizations. She loves gospel, jazz and country music. She enjoys community service, traveling, writing and making handcrafted spa products as part of her self-care and pampering rituals. Janice is currently a resident of the Garden State of New Jersey.